Numbers Made Simple

Numbers Made Simple

Accounting and Finance for the One-Person Business – Step-by-step basics of bookkeeping, P&L, and cash flow

Evelyn Hawthorne

Mindful Pages

Published in 2026

ISBN: 9789374122877 (PB)
ISBN: 9789374128220 (eBook)

Published by

Mindful Pages
Imprint of Alpha Editions LLC
312 W. 2nd St #1834
Casper, WY 82601, USA

This book was developed using advanced writing tools to support the drafting and ideation process. All content has been thoughtfully curated, refined, and reviewed to ensure quality and relevance.

Content

Introduction

The Quiet Power of a Small Ledger

A curious paradox haunts the world of one-person businesses. A designer doubles her hours, chasing every lead with relentless zeal, only to feel poorer at the month's end. A coach adds three new clients, celebrates the wins, yet watches her bank balance shrink. Again and again, the problem masquerades as "not enough work" or "not enough growth." In truth, it is usually something quieter, subtler, and far more solvable: the numbers were never speaking clearly. A business can thrive or wither not on the size of its pipeline but on the clarity of its ledger.

Here lies the quiet revolution at the heart of this book: a freelancer, consultant, or small creative can sometimes double their effective revenue without sending a single extra invoice—simply by learning, at last, where the real profit hides and where cash slips away unnoticed. Growth, for most one-person businesses, is less about acceleration than about illumination. Once you see the true contours of your money, choices sharpen, waste shrinks, and suddenly you are running not faster, but freer.

This book begins with that promise: modest in appearance, radical in consequence. No sweeping financial theory, no dizzying spreadsheets, no jargon meant to impress accountants. Instead, a humane routine, compact enough to live inside a single hour a week, yet powerful enough to turn confusion into command. A routine that replaces anxiety with evidence, and transforms financial fog into decisions that feel almost inevitable.

The Paradox of Growth and Clarity

The mythology of entrepreneurship insists that hustle solves all. More clients, more projects, more hours at the desk—that is the drumbeat. Yet history, both distant and recent, whispers a different lesson. During the early days of industrial trade, merchants who prospered were not those who shouted loudest in the market, but those who kept the most careful books. The Venetian traders who mastered double-entry accounting in the fifteenth century could outmanoeuvre rivals by sheer foresight, spotting weaknesses and opportunities invisible to others. Their ledgers became not only records but instruments of strategy.

Fast forward to the present, and the pattern endures. In a world where software promises automation and dashboards overwhelm with colour and charts, most small business owners still drown in noise. They confuse revenue for profit, cash for confidence, and growth for health. The result is financial whiplash: good weeks that leave them broke, strong months followed by sudden droughts. The error is not laziness but orientation. They are chasing growth to patch over clarity gaps. Numbers remain something distant, outsourced, or dreaded.

This book argues the opposite: clarity comes first. Clean books prevent the very crises that frantic growth attempts to solve. By confronting your numbers directly—simply, consistently, and with purpose—you discover that the most urgent business questions can be answered with surprising speed. Can I pay myself this week? Can I afford that investment? Which clients nourish profit, and which quietly bleed it dry? These are the questions a ledger—small, disciplined, and honest—can resolve.

A Ledger as Compass

Think of the ledger not as a dusty archive but as a compass. It does not tell you where you have been, but where you are turning. It points not north or south but towards clarity or confusion. Every week, you face choices: whether to take on one more client, whether to raise a rate, whether to renew a subscription or retire it. Without numbers, you are guessing in the dark. With numbers—even the simplest—your options acquire contour, weight, consequence.

There is a motif that will run quietly through these pages: the loop. Capture, categorise, compare, decide. These four verbs form the rhythm of a solo business that wishes to thrive. Capture what flows in and out. Categorise it in buckets that make sense to you. Compare against last week, last month, last project. Decide, always, something small but tangible. The loop is unglamorous, almost humble—but once named and practised, it becomes a living operating system for your business.

The beauty lies in proportion. A one-person company does not need the sprawling architecture of a multinational. You do not need to predict ten years into the future, nor reconcile thousands of transactions each quarter. What you need is density of signal. A handful of metrics, curated for meaning rather than volume, can illuminate far more than endless dashboards. The trick is to stop mistaking complexity for control.

Urgency and Timelessness

Why is this subject urgent now? Because the one-person business has never been more common, nor more precarious. Millions across the globe are building careers that resist traditional employment: freelancers, coaches, consultants, independent creators. Technology makes it possible; culture makes it desirable. Yet finance remains the unspoken weak link. Creative independence often comes shackled to financial anxiety. The volatility of income, the confusion of taxes, the blur between personal and business accounts—these problems corrode not only wealth but confidence.

And yet the subject is timeless. Long before corporations and auditors, humans have used small ledgers to survive and prosper. Farmers tallied yields against seed. Shopkeepers noted credits and debts in smudged notebooks. Soldiers recorded pay owed and rations distributed. The ledger, in miniature, has always been about dignity and foresight. It reminds us that prosperity is not only the product of what we earn, but of what we perceive and decide with clarity.

The urgency and timelessness converge in this book. We are not inventing new principles so much as recovering old ones—recasting them for the age of Stripe accounts, PayPal transfers, and cloud folders. The principle remains: control flows not from hustle but from seeing clearly.

What This Book Offers

This book is not a textbook of accounting. You will not find lengthy digressions into statutory compliance, nor the algebra of corporate finance. What you will find is a set of practices built for the scale and shape of a one-person business. Each chapter is a tool: a way to design accounts that feel intuitive, a ritual of weekly closure that replaces dread with calm, a method for reading a profit and loss statement as if it were a story, not a riddle.

At the centre lies a promise: you can transform how you feel about money in your business, not by becoming an accountant, but by adopting a few deliberate rituals. In 45 minutes a week, you can turn chaos into pattern. You can spot which projects nourish you and which hollow you out. You can prevent overdrafts before they occur, instead of apologising to your bank after the fact. You can price with confidence, not because you have mastered psychology, but because the evidence supports you.

And beyond these practicalities lies something subtler but more profound: a sense of calm. When the numbers speak, the noise subsides. You stop chasing every lead as if it were salvation. You stop fearing the taxman as if he were a predator. You begin to trust yourself with money—not because you hope, but because you know.

Forward Tension

The chapters ahead will return repeatedly to a question: what decisions must your numbers answer? This is the fulcrum of the book. Not every metric matters. Not every report deserves your attention. Numbers that cannot change a decision are ornamental at best, distracting at worst. Our task is to strip away, to refine, to leave you with a small ledger that speaks directly to the decisions that matter: Can I pay myself? Can I afford this? What truly made money? What drained it? What changed since last week?

But this raises deeper provocations. If money is now speaking to you with clarity, will you listen? What will you do when the numbers reveal that your favourite client is also your least profitable? What happens when the data shows that raising your price would lose one client but double your margin? Will you trust the evidence enough to act, or will you retreat to the comfort of hustle?

The quiet power of a small ledger is not in the numbers alone, but in the courage they demand. Clarity is unsettling before it is liberating. Yet once you cross that threshold, decisions feel almost obvious. The chase for growth fades. The sense of drift dissolves. You begin to steer with intent, guided by evidence, not anxiety.

So let us begin, not with data, but with decisions. Not with the illusion of growth, but with the discipline of clarity. Your ledger is waiting—not as a burden, but as a compass. And once you learn to read it, you may find that freedom in business is less about doing more and more about finally seeing what has been true all along.

Chapter 1
Start with Decisions, Not Data

A consultant I once met kept immaculate records. Every receipt was scanned, every invoice numbered, every coffee charged to a client neatly logged. His accounting software was a marvel of colour-coded precision. And yet, he confessed, he felt perpetually behind. He did not know if he could afford a new laptop. He could not say with confidence whether his last workshop had actually made him money. The irony was brutal: the man had more data than he could ever need, and not a shred of clarity where it mattered.

This is the quiet trap of modern business: mistaking accumulation for understanding. The tools at our disposal promise dashboards, charts, exports, trendlines. They seduce us into thinking that if we just gather enough information, truth will emerge. But clarity rarely scales with volume. More often, it is buried under it. For a one-person business, the central task is not to collect more, but to ask better: to decide first what questions your numbers must answer, and only then to assemble the reports that matter.

That distinction—questions before data—is not cosmetic. It is existential. A solo operator cannot afford to squander attention on ornamental metrics. Every hour spent wrangling spreadsheets is an hour not spent creating, serving, or selling. The purpose of your books is not to impress an accountant or decorate a dashboard; it is to serve decisions. And if a report cannot change a decision, it is not essential. It may be pretty, but it is superfluous.

The five weekly questions that anchor this chapter are deceptively simple: Can I pay myself? Can I afford this? What made money? What bled cash? What changed since last week? That is all. Five questions, no more. Each one can be mapped to a single report or metric, no sprawling charts required. The genius of starting here is discipline: it protects you from the temptation to build for display rather than use. You are not creating an accounting cathedral; you are building a shed that keeps the rain off. Function before form, clarity before gloss.

To grasp why this matters, consider the alternative. Many small operators begin with software. They sign up for tools brimming with integrations, widgets, and dashboards. At first, the novelty delights: colourful graphs, endless toggles, real-time feeds. But slowly, the shine dulls. Reports proliferate without purpose. Weekly rituals bloat into chores. The user drowns in noise. What began as empowerment becomes a burden. Starting with questions, by contrast, inverts the process. It is not "what can the tool show me?" but "what do I need to decide?" That inversion changes everything.

And here another distinction arises: lagging versus leading. Results versus drivers. The problem with relying only on results—revenue, profit, the lines that appear on a monthly statement—is that they tell you what has already happened. They are history, not foresight. Useful, yes, but inert. A designer who looks only at last month's profit will not see the pipeline drying up. A coach who celebrates record revenue may not notice that client utilisation has dropped dangerously low. Drivers, by contrast—average selling price, pipeline health, delivery hours booked—offer a glimpse around the corner.

The discipline, then, is cadence. Weekly, you review the drivers. Monthly, you review the results. Together, they form a rhythm that steadies you. You are no longer jerked from elation to despair by one big invoice landing or a sudden drought in work. You can see patterns forming early, and correct course before crisis. This rhythm protects your attention: no more whiplash, no more frantic course-correcting. Instead, you gain the confidence of foresight, the ability to act before the cliff-edge.

Yet cadence and discipline mean little without the right lens. That lens is what we might call *signal density*: the smallest slice of data that still improves a choice. Paradoxically, micro-samples—ten invoices, three proposals—often tell you more than a sprawling export of hundreds of lines. A handful of carefully chosen points can reveal pricing weaknesses, client fit, or seasonal drift. The exercise, always, is pruning. Drop columns that do not inform action. Remove metrics that flatter but do not direct. One coach who cut three such metrics found her pricing discipline sharpened immediately; she no longer hid behind vanity ratios. The lesson: less data, stronger action.

In practice, the pruning feels almost subversive. We are conditioned to think more numbers equal more control. But numbers are not neutral; they carry cognitive weight. Each extra column is another claim on your attention, another whisper in the noise. The courage to strip away is itself a decision. What remains is denser, sharper, more potent. What remains speaks.

From these principles emerges the loop that will serve as this book's spine: Capture → Categorise → Compare → Decide. Four verbs, bound tightly, each with limits. Capture what comes in; categorise it with clear rules; compare it to a reference point; decide something tangible. The loop is engineered to finish in under forty-five minutes each week. It is not meant to be perfect, but complete. Once named, it becomes a shared language—a way to spot where breakdowns occur. Did you fail to capture? Did categorisation slip? Was comparison lazy? Did you stop short of a decision? With the loop, diagnosis becomes immediate.

This is not bookkeeping as drudgery, nor finance as compliance. It is rhythm, habit, a cycle that sustains itself. The loop is both safety net and compass: safety net because it catches errors before they metastasise; compass because it always orients back to decisions. And in naming it, we strip away the mystique of accounting. Finance is not a labyrinth. It is a loop.

This chapter, then, begins with a simple invitation: invert the order. Start not with what you can track, but with what you must decide. Build not dashboards, but answers. Recognise the limits of results, and pair them with the foresight of drivers. Embrace signal density, not signal noise. And adopt the loop as a rhythm you can sustain, not a burden you will abandon.

What follows will not be grand theory but practical scaffolding. You will learn the five questions that matter most, the cadence that protects your attention, the discipline of pruning, and the loop that holds it all together. Each element is small, almost humble. But taken together, they redraw the relationship between you and your business.

The truth is simple but sharp: numbers are not the point. Decisions are. And once you begin to treat them as such, the fog lifts. The ledger becomes a companion, not a tyrant. And you may discover, to your surprise, that running on evidence feels lighter, freer, even exhilarating. What waits ahead is not more work, but less—because now, finally, your numbers know where to point.

What Questions Must Your Numbers Answer?

One of the great ironies of modern work is that many of the most industrious solo operators are awash with figures yet deprived of clarity. Their software delivers dashboards that sparkle with colour, their inboxes overflow with reports, and their bank feeds stream transactions by the hundred. But when asked a simple question—*Can you pay yourself next week?*—they hesitate. The noise of data has replaced the substance of knowledge. In the end, it is not the quantity of numbers at your disposal that matters, but the sharpness of the questions you put to them.

The history of commerce offers countless reminders. Renaissance merchants who pioneered double-entry accounting did not begin with data for its own sake; they began with practical questions. Could they settle debts with their creditors? Which voyages yielded true profit once costs were stripped out? Which partners were trustworthy? Their ledgers were not monuments to thoroughness but working tools, instruments of decision. In their restraint lay their strength: a merchant could glance at a few lines of ink and know whether to invest in another ship or stay ashore. Centuries later, the principle remains unchanged.

For the one-person business, the questions are more modest but no less consequential. Each week, there are five inquiries to be made—small enough to fit on a single card, weighty enough to direct the course of a livelihood. They are not abstract prompts but practical thresholds, guardrails that prevent drift. *Can I pay myself? Can I afford this? What made money? What bled cash? What changed since last week?* If you can answer these five, you are running on evidence, not assumption. If you cannot, every decision is guesswork dressed as confidence.

Consider the first: *Can I pay myself?* This is the anchor question, the one too often neglected in favour of revenue figures that flatter but deceive. A freelancer who celebrates a £10,000 invoice may still struggle to cover their own needs if payment arrives late, or if costs have quietly swallowed margin. To know whether you can pay yourself is to bridge the gap between headline numbers and lived reality. It is not enough to know what has been billed; you must know what is liquid, what is free of obligations, what is yours to draw without destabilising the business.

Next, *Can I afford this?*—a question that guards against impulsive commitments. Every one-person enterprise faces choices about tools, subscriptions, subcontractors, even office chairs. The temptation to rationalise every purchase as "an investment" is strong. But the discipline is sharper: affordability is not a matter of desire but of evidence. This question maps to a single report of available free cash, and to a forecast no longer than a fortnight. The answer may be yes, no, or not yet. In all cases, clarity beats hope.

Then comes *What made money?* Here the lens narrows to contribution. Did that coaching package, after accounting for preparation time and materials, truly return a profit? Did that design project pay more than it cost to deliver? The question insists on separating revenue from profitability. It exposes the common illusion of "busy but broke" enterprises, where full calendars conceal thin margins. A single report, structured to show gross profit by client or service line, can deliver the answer. The discipline is liberating: you discover which work deserves expansion, and which ought to be retired.

Alongside it stands its shadow: *What bled cash?* No system is without leaks. Sometimes it is an underpriced project; sometimes it is software subscriptions that linger long after usefulness fades. For many, the slow bleed of small recurring costs does more damage than a single extravagant expense. This question brings gravity to outflows, insisting on ranking them by their effect on profit. A simple list—sorted, not sprawling—can be enough to trigger decisive pruning. The point is not guilt but sovereignty: to know where your money slips away is to reclaim the power to stop it.

The fifth and final question—*What changed since last week?*—seems almost trivial, but it is the heartbeat of vigilance. Change is where risk and opportunity reside. A sudden dip in proposals sent, an unexpected jump in expenses, a shift in average invoice size: these small movements often forecast larger swings ahead. By training yourself to notice change rather than chase absolute numbers, you catch patterns early. It is the difference between steering gradually and swerving in panic. A simple week-on-week comparison, no more than a page, grounds the answer.

These five questions form a purpose-built stack: compact, sufficient, disciplined. They resist the temptation to build dashboards bristling with indicators that look impressive but alter nothing. Any report that does not change a decision is decoration. And decoration, in the life of a solo operator, is costly. It consumes time, scatters attention, and often confuses more than it clarifies. The act of scoping questions first is an act of respect—for your time, for your focus, for the business you are building.

The intellectual appeal of this approach lies in its austerity. It mirrors principles found in fields as diverse as science and philosophy: begin not with data collection, but with the framing of inquiry. Galileo did not begin by measuring everything; he asked precise questions about motion. A good ethnographer does not transcribe entire societies; they pursue themes. Clarity of question determines clarity of answer. So it is with the ledger: the discipline of scoping questions protects you from the tyranny of excess.

There will always be voices arguing for more: more metrics, more reports, more "visibility." The corporate world, with its layers of management, requires sprawling dashboards to co-ordinate teams and justify decisions. But the one-person business lives by different rules. What is expansive in a corporation becomes suffocating for an individual. For you, the measure of rigour is not quantity but precision. You need just enough to decide, no more.

And yet, this restraint provokes unease. Many find comfort in abundance, mistaking the proliferation of numbers for control. To strip down feels risky, almost negligent. But the opposite is true. The lean stack is stronger precisely because it points relentlessly to action.

Each report is tethered to a choice: pay yourself or wait; buy or defer; expand or contract; continue or stop; adjust or hold steady. Decisions are the currency of business. Numbers are valuable only insofar as they serve them.

The deeper question, of course, lingers beneath: do we have the courage to act on what we see? It is one thing to know a project lost money; it is another to retire it, or to raise a price and risk losing a client. It is one thing to see that your expenses bleed cash; another to cancel the subscriptions that offer comfort. Numbers answer questions, but they do not make choices. That burden—and that power—remains yours.

What emerges, then, is both a tool and a test. The tool: five questions, answered weekly, mapping neatly to five reports. The test: whether you will let those answers shape your behaviour. For in the end, the value of clarity is not in the knowing, but in the deciding. And that is where this chapter turns next: how to distinguish the results that lag from the drivers that lead, and how to weave them into a rhythm that protects your attention from the shocks of surprise.

The questions, then, are only the beginning. What matters is how you live with their answers.

Lagging vs Leading: Seeing Around Corners

A designer once told me he felt like he was forever steering his business by looking in the rear-view mirror. Each month he'd receive his profit and loss statement, carefully generated by his accounting software, and only then would he discover whether he had actually made money. By that point, the projects that caused the problem were finished, the invoices long sent, and the choices already locked in. The numbers arrived not as guidance but as a verdict—too late to help, just in time to sting.

This is the paradox at the heart of small business finance. The reports most readily available are lagging indicators: revenue, profit, cash on hand. They tell you what has already happened, but they cannot warn you of what lies ahead. If you steer only by them, you live in a constant state of reaction. One month feels like a triumph, the next a disaster. The result is emotional whiplash, a frantic oscillation between overconfidence and despair. The figures may be accurate, but their timing is cruel.

The antidote lies in distinguishing results from drivers—lagging from leading. Results are the record: what you billed, what you spent, what you kept. Drivers are the forces that shape those results: how many proposals you sent, how many hours were billable, what your average selling price was. Drivers change first. Results follow. To treat them as equivalent is to confuse cause with effect, motion with outcome. But to pair them in the right rhythm—a weekly review of drivers, a monthly review of results—is to give yourself the gift of foresight.

Consider a coach whose pipeline consists of exploratory calls with prospective clients. If she tracks only her monthly revenue, she sees the outcome too late: either a good month or a lean one. But if she reviews the number of exploratory calls each week, she sees movement before it hardens into results. A dip in calls today forecasts a revenue dip in six weeks. A sudden surge predicts a cash bump ahead. The leading indicator becomes a lighthouse; she can prepare rather than panic.

The same holds for a freelance designer. His monthly income fluctuates wildly, driven by the timing of projects. If he looks only at revenue, he experiences feast and famine as random fate. But if he tracks his average project value and utilisation rate weekly, the fog clears. A fall in average value hints at underpricing or weak positioning. A slip in utilisation shows under-booking. Both are warnings he can act on before they turn into a negative bottom line. Drivers, observed weekly, give him time to steer.

The deeper significance here is philosophical. Human beings crave certainty, yet most of the data we cling to is retrospective. We are like generals who review the last battle with exquisite precision while the next one gathers at the border. The discipline of distinguishing lagging from leading indicators is a discipline of humility. It is the recognition that to see around corners, you must watch the moving parts, not the finished scorecard.

The value of cadence cannot be overstated. A weekly review of drivers is brief but vital. It catches subtle changes, much as a physician takes a pulse: small fluctuations that reveal the state of the system before crises erupt. A monthly review of results, by contrast, is reflective. It consolidates, reveals patterns, tests whether the drivers you tracked are indeed the right ones. The two cadences complement each other. Weekly is for steering; monthly is for sense-making. Together, they form a rhythm that stabilises attention and reduces panic.

Without this rhythm, small business owners often pinball between overreaction and neglect. A slow week becomes a cause for existential dread. A single large payment lulls them into false security. Decisions are made in extremes, not in balance. But with the rhythm in place, the noise flattens. You see that a slow week is a blip, not a collapse. You notice that one large invoice does not offset a weak pipeline. The cadence restores perspective.

This distinction between leading and lagging is not confined to finance. In medicine, symptoms are lagging, but biomarkers are leading. In education, exam results are lagging, but attendance and engagement are leading. In fitness, weight on the scale is lagging, but hours of sleep and training intensity are leading. Everywhere, the same principle holds: the measures that matter most arrive too late to change, unless you learn to track their precursors.

For the solo business, the lesson is both practical and existential. Practical, because knowing which metric to watch weekly can prevent cash crunches and pricing errors. Existential, because it changes your relationship with time. You no longer live at the mercy of past results; you live in anticipation, able to adjust before consequences land. This shift, subtle as it seems, alters not just decisions but psychology. Anxiety ebbs, replaced by a steadier confidence rooted in foresight.

And yet, a tension remains. Leading indicators are predictive, but not certain. They warn, but they do not guarantee. A full pipeline may still collapse if proposals are weak. High utilisation may hide underpricing. This ambiguity can frustrate. But it is also the point. The role of a leading indicator is not to promise the future, but to illuminate the present forces shaping it. It gives you a chance to intervene, not a guarantee of success.

The challenge, then, is choice. Which drivers truly matter? Which are noise disguised as signal? To answer wrongly is to create busywork, tracking indicators that never map to outcomes. To answer wisely is to create a feedback loop of extraordinary power. The art lies in pruning to a handful of leading indicators that, together, explain most of your results. More than that, and the clarity dissolves. Less, and you risk blindness.

The question, finally, is one of trust. Will you learn to trust the drivers before the results confirm them? Will you act on the warning in the pipeline dip, or will you wait until revenue collapses to believe it? Will you raise your prices when average value slips, or will you wait for the P&L to punish you? To work with leading indicators is to embrace a kind of faith in evidence, incomplete but compelling.

And so the discipline of seeing around corners demands courage. It asks you to look at motion rather than destination, to accept ambiguity in exchange for foresight, to act before certainty arrives. Many will hesitate, preferring the comfort of the verdict, even if it comes too late. But those who adopt the rhythm—weekly drivers, monthly results—discover a steadier path. Their attention is protected, their surprises fewer, their choices sharper.

What remains unresolved, and what will test you in practice, is the balance: how few leading indicators are enough, how much faith to place in them, and how to resist the lure of reacting only when the verdict is in. For to see around corners is not to know the future, but to be ready for it. And readiness, for the one-person business, is often the difference between calm and chaos.

Small Data, Big Signal

In 2019, a small creative agency nearly bankrupted itself not through extravagance but through analysis. Determined to become more "data-driven," its founder exported every transaction, every timesheet entry, every client invoice into sprawling spreadsheets. They built dashboards with dozens of metrics, convinced that visibility meant control. Yet the opposite happened. Drowned in columns, paralysed by graphs, they lost the thread. Decisions slowed, attention scattered, and the one number that mattered—profit—remained elusive. The irony was brutal: more data produced less clarity.

The story is not unique. Many solo operators and small businesses are seduced by the promise of "big data." They collect endlessly—sales funnels, marketing clicks, tool usage rates, ten-year comparisons of categories they barely use. Yet the signal that might actually change a choice is often hidden in plain sight, smothered by volume. The paradox is striking: *less data, interpreted with precision, is often more powerful than mountains of information analysed poorly.*

The principle is what we might call *signal density*: the smallest view of numbers that still improves a choice. It is not minimalism for its own sake. It is not about austerity or anti-technology nostalgia. It is about efficiency of insight. Every additional data point consumes attention, and attention is the scarcest resource a one-person business possesses. The question, then, is not *what can I measure?* but *what do I need to see to act differently?*

Consider pricing. A consultant once tracked more than twenty different metrics related to her projects: average hours per client, time per meeting, discounts given, software allocations, even incidental travel expenses. But when she pruned her reporting to just three—average selling price, contribution margin per client, and hours delivered versus hours billed—her behaviour changed. She spotted immediately which packages were consistently underpriced. She noticed which clients consumed far more hours than billed. Within three months, she had raised fees on two services and cut one offering entirely. Revenue rose, stress fell. The other seventeen metrics, she realised, had never once altered a decision.

Micro-samples often reveal more than sprawling exports. Take invoices. Analysing ten recent invoices for average payment times can often tell you more about your cash flow than exporting two years of payment history. The smaller set is fresher, easier to interpret, and closer to the decision at hand: *Do I need to change my invoicing terms?* Similarly, looking at the last three proposals sent can teach you more about your current pipeline strength than studying every proposal since you began freelancing. The relevance of the data is heightened precisely because it is narrow and immediate.

This runs counter to the cultural mood, which equates comprehensiveness with seriousness. Corporations employ analysts whose job is to mine vast datasets, unearth correlations, and justify strategies with reams of evidence. But a solo operator is not a corporation. You do not need a hundred rows of export to decide whether to raise a price. You need a clear view of whether your last handful of sales held their margin. Big data is impressive. Small data is decisive.

The danger of excess is not only distraction but distortion. When too many columns compete for attention, you gravitate toward those that flatter rather than those that matter. Vanity metrics—total followers, total billings without costs, number of enquiries regardless of conversion—seduce the ego while leaving the business exposed. The pruning exercise is therefore an act of intellectual honesty. Which numbers make you behave differently, and which merely decorate the page?

Philosophically, this is the same problem that plagues human knowledge more broadly. We are surrounded by unprecedented information, yet wisdom does not grow at the same pace. The historian T.S. Eliot's lament—"Where is the wisdom we have lost in knowledge? Where is the knowledge we have lost in information?"—rings truer today than when it was written. The principle of signal density is a direct response: not everything that can be counted counts, and not everything that counts can be counted. The discipline is to choose.

A striking example comes from a small design studio that once tracked nine different marketing metrics: impressions, click-through rates, likes, shares, open rates, unsubscribes, leads, conversions, and cost per click. The founder admitted, however, that she rarely acted on most of them. What changed her behaviour was tracking just two: cost per qualified lead and average project size closed. By reducing to those, she made faster decisions on which campaigns to keep and which to abandon. She was no longer dazzled by surface-level engagement but focused directly on what improved profit. The pruning stripped away noise and surfaced leverage.

Signal density does not mean ignoring context. It means sharpening it. Small samples are not chosen at random but curated to capture the essence of what matters now. For example, a two-week rolling view of expenses may not show long-term patterns, but it tells you immediately whether recurring costs are creeping higher. A snapshot of your last five client projects may not provide exhaustive statistics, but it reveals whether your recent pricing aligns with the time you actually worked. By narrowing scope, you bring immediacy and relevance into sharper focus.

The counterargument, of course, is that larger datasets provide robustness. And in corporate finance, where millions of pounds are at stake, this is true. But in a one-person business, the problem is rarely statistical error; it is interpretive paralysis. You do not need 1,000 samples to know that a client who consumes 40 hours of unbilled time is unprofitable. One or two examples suffice. You do not need five years of expense history to see that software subscriptions are ballooning; last month's statement makes it obvious. The law of small numbers, in this case, works to your advantage: it speeds decision-making.

The philosophical shift is profound. Instead of chasing completeness, you accept that a small, sharp picture is more useful than a vast, blurred one. This acceptance is liberating. It reframes financial management not as an endless trawl through data but as a series of tightly scoped checks. What do I need to know to decide, today? Anything more is luxury.

Yet the practice is not without risk. Small samples can mislead if chosen poorly. A freelancer who looks only at her last two clients may draw the wrong conclusion about pricing if those clients were outliers. A coach who examines only one delayed invoice may panic unnecessarily about payment reliability. The discipline, then, is to balance smallness with representativeness. Enough data to see a real pattern, not so much that the pattern is lost.

This balance is what makes the concept of pruning so vital. By consciously removing low-value columns, you are not rejecting data itself but clarifying its hierarchy. You acknowledge that not all numbers are equal, and you elevate those that matter most. It is not a rejection of complexity but a reordering of it. The reward is stronger action: fewer numbers, sharper moves.

And here the motif returns: the smallest view that still improves a choice. That is the test. If a metric does not alter your behaviour, it does not belong in your weekly stack. If a column exists only to reassure you that you are "tracking everything," it is excess. The stack you build is not ornamental; it is surgical.

The unresolved question, however, is one of courage. Do you trust yourself enough to strip away? Can you tolerate the discomfort of fewer numbers, even if the few you keep speak more plainly? The temptation to return to excess will always be there, reinforced by culture, software, and ego. To resist it is to embrace not ignorance but focus.

Small data, wielded with discipline, is not a retreat from rigour but its highest form. For the one-person business, it is the difference between drowning in analysis and acting with conviction. And yet, the tension lingers: what if the signal you prune away was the one that could have warned you? What if the simplicity you embrace blinds you to nuance?

That question is not easily dismissed. It is the risk that shadows every act of focus. But without the pruning, the alternative is paralysis. And for a solo operator, paralysis is often costlier than error. The signal you can act on today is stronger than the dataset you will never finish interpreting. The discipline is to choose—and to trust that in choosing less, you might finally see more.

The Four-Step Finance Loop

A photographer once confessed that her books terrified her. Each tax season she would hand over a shoebox of receipts to her accountant and brace for the verdict. The months between were a blur of guesswork: sometimes she overpaid herself and ended the quarter short on cash, sometimes she hoarded money unnecessarily and starved her own household. What struck me most was her language. She spoke as though finance were an inscrutable ritual performed once a year by a priestly figure. Yet when pressed, she admitted she already had the tools—bank feeds, invoicing apps, even a basic spreadsheet. What she lacked was not data but rhythm.

This absence of rhythm is what paralyses so many one-person businesses. Without a simple, repeatable process, financial work becomes a sporadic emergency. Spikes of panic, followed by long stretches of neglect. The alternative, however, is deceptively modest: a loop so compact it can be completed in under forty-five minutes a week, yet strong enough to keep a business aligned. Capture. Categorise. Compare. Decide. Four verbs, stitched together into a self-contained circuit. A loop, not a labyrinth.

What makes this structure powerful is not complexity but containment. Each step has boundaries. Each step has a purpose. And together, they transform finance from an open-ended slog into a finite ritual—something you can start and finish, week after week, without dread. The loop's genius lies in its closure: you always know when you are done.

The first movement is *Capture*. This is the gathering stage, the sweeping of the surface so nothing escapes. Every inflow and outflow—bank transactions, PayPal charges, Stripe deposits, cash withdrawals—enters a single inbox. The principle is simple: you cannot analyse what you cannot see. Capture is not yet about judgement, only collection. A designer who downloads her bank feed each Friday or a coach who syncs Stripe into a single folder is practising capture. It is mechanical, finite, and time-capped. Ten minutes suffices. Anything more is drift.

The second verb is *Categorise*. Here, decisions begin. Each transaction must find a home: earning, delivering, or running. Direct cost or overhead. Business or personal. The discipline is to use rules, not memory. If the same subscription recurs monthly, automate its destination. If a client always pays under the same reference, pre-fill it. The danger at this stage is not error but fatigue. Memory is costly; rules are cheap. By enforcing rules, categorisation shrinks from a guessing game into a repeatable habit. Again, time-capped: fifteen minutes.

The third step is *Compare*. Numbers in isolation are inert. Only by placing them against a reference—last week, last month, last quarter—do they reveal meaning. Comparison surfaces change: the rise in outflows, the dip in utilisation, the improvement in average selling price. It is the pivot from record-keeping to insight. The comparison need not be elaborate. A simple side-by-side table or chart suffices. What matters is that it shows movement, not just totals. Ten minutes here can reveal more than hours spent staring at raw figures.

And then comes the final verb: *Decide*. Without this, the loop collapses into bookkeeping for its own sake. Decision is the point at which numbers become action. Each week, you identify one spend to stop, one price to test, one invoice to chase. Small, concrete, executable. The cumulative effect of these micro-decisions is profound. A client who consistently pays late is dropped. A subscription that adds no visible value is cancelled. A service that bleeds margin is repriced. Over months, these tiny decisions compound into a stronger business. Fifteen minutes, no more. Decide, log it, close the loop.

The loop is not only efficient; it is diagnostic. By naming its four steps, you gain a shared language to identify breakdowns. If your numbers feel unreliable, perhaps capture is incomplete. If reports look messy, categorisation has slipped. If you feel you are drowning in data without meaning, comparison is missing. If nothing changes despite review, decision is absent. Each breakdown is specific, and each has a remedy. This precision prevents the spiral of "I'm just bad with money." You are not bad; the loop has a kink. Straighten it, and the cycle resumes.

What is striking here is how universal the logic of loops is. In biology, the body survives by feedback loops—capture input, categorise it, compare to baseline, decide on a response. In engineering, control systems run on loops of sensing, processing, and acting. Finance, too, obeys the same principle. What matters is not that you see everything once, but that you see enough regularly. The loop transforms finance from sporadic crisis into continuous feedback.

A striking case came from a freelance copywriter who adopted this method. She used to spend hours each quarter in a frenzy of reconciliation, only to emerge exhausted and none the wiser. Once she adopted the loop—forty minutes every Friday morning—her behaviour changed. Capture: bank feed pulled into her accounting app. Categorise: rules cleaned up 80 per cent automatically. Compare: a one-page sheet showing week-on-week shifts. Decide: one action logged in a notebook. Within three months she discovered she was undercharging one retainer client by 30 per cent. Within six months she had pruned three unnecessary tools. For the first time, she described her finances as "calm."

Yet a tension remains. The loop is deceptively simple, but simplicity can be unsettling. Many equate sophistication with value: complex dashboards, thick reports, elaborate reconciliations. The loop feels almost too small. Can forty-five minutes really suffice? The evidence suggests it can. The discipline is not in breadth but in repetition. A loop sustained weekly will outperform a marathon of catch-up every quarter. Like fitness, small consistent sessions trump heroic binges.

There is also a philosophical undercurrent. Loops impose limits. They force closure. They resist the endless temptation to keep tweaking, keep analysing, keep searching for a perfect picture. In a culture addicted to more—more data, more metrics, more dashboards—the loop says: enough. Four steps, forty-five minutes, finished. The act of closure is not laziness but respect for time.

Still, the loop asks a final question of its user: will you trust it? Will you resist the urge to add steps, extend sessions, complicate categories? Will you accept that imperfection repeated is stronger than perfection attempted rarely? For the one-person business, this may be the hardest discipline of all.

Capture. Categorise. Compare. Decide. Four verbs that, repeated weekly, can turn finance from a source of dread into a source of direction. But only if you honour the loop as it stands: bounded, repeatable, finite. The challenge is not in learning the steps, but in keeping faith with them when the lure of complexity returns. And so the loop becomes not just a method but a mirror: will you keep it small, or will you let it sprawl? The answer will decide more than your numbers—it will decide your calm.

Chapter 2
A Simple Chart of Accounts That Thinks Like You

An independent architect once told me that she spent more time arguing with her accounting software than with her clients. Every purchase demanded a choice: was that new graphics tablet "office equipment" or "design tools"? Was the subcontractor's invoice "labour" or "professional services"? Each decision felt arbitrary, a distraction from the work she actually cared about. By year's end her reports were littered with inconsistent categories. The irony was cruel: her books were detailed, but they told her nothing useful about her business.

This is a problem more common than most realise. The standard chart of accounts—the master list of categories into which every transaction must fall—was not designed with one-person businesses in mind. It is a legacy of corporate accounting, where sprawling hierarchies and tax compliance drive the structure. For a solo operator, it is overkill. The categories proliferate, the language feels alien, and the reports produced rarely answer the questions that matter most. The result is friction: transactions pile up uncategorised, or worse, are shoved into whatever slot feels least wrong. Accuracy slips, confidence erodes, and clarity is lost.

The paradox is this: more categories often lead to less accuracy. When every decision feels hair-splitting, consistency collapses. By contrast, fewer buckets—designed to mirror the way you actually think about your business—improve both speed and precision. The power lies in stripping down, not bulking up. A chart of accounts that thinks like you aligns to the natural flow of your work: earning, delivering, running. Three broad streams, each a "default destination" for transactions. Suddenly, categorisation ceases to be a guessing game. Every inflow and outflow finds its home almost automatically. The result is not only cleaner books but reports that feel intuitive, trustworthy, and alive.

At the heart of this lies a deeper point: structure shapes perception. A poorly designed chart of accounts distorts your view of reality. If you misclassify subcontractors as overhead instead of direct costs, you obscure the contribution margin of your projects—the line that reveals whether a job was truly profitable. If you bury software tools in a vague catch-all, you cannot see whether they support delivery or merely inflate running costs. Categories are not neutral; they are lenses. They decide what is visible and what remains hidden. And hidden numbers mislead.

The difference matters because contribution margin is the fulcrum of strategy for a one-person business. It is the line that distinguishes between projects worth repeating and projects that hollow you out. Get it wrong, and you may celebrate revenue while bleeding profit. Get it right, and you have a compass for pricing, client selection, and resource allocation. A simple reclassification—grey expenses moved to their rightful place—can transform the way you understand your own work. What once looked like slim profit may reveal itself as robust; what once seemed promising may turn out to be loss-making. The clarity is not cosmetic but strategic.

But clarity is fragile if your personal and business finances are entangled. Many solos blur the line, not out of negligence but out of convenience. A coffee for a client meeting ends up on the same card as groceries. A personal subscription is occasionally claimed as a business tool. At first, it seems harmless. Over time, the distortions grow. Tax estimates inflate or shrink unpredictably. Cash balances deceive. Anxiety creeps in. The fix is not perfectionism but guardrails: two accounts, one inbox for captures, simple rules that protect you without demanding obsession. You do not need to chase flawless separation; you need pragmatic boundaries that preserve trust in your numbers. Guardrails, not guilt.

What emerges is a finance system that lowers cognitive load. Instead of asking, *Am I doing this right?* every time a transaction appears, you know its natural destination. Instead of panicking at tax season, you know that business and personal flows are sufficiently distinct to produce a reliable estimate. And with this trust, attention returns to where it belongs: making decisions, not fighting categories.

There is another layer often overlooked: naming conventions. The way you label vendors, projects, and transactions determines whether your records remain usable over time. Inconsistent naming—"Adobe," "Adobe Inc.," "Adobe Systems"—creates needless friction when searching later. A disciplined pattern—always "Vendor: Adobe"—unlocks searchability and comparability. Memo tags serve the same role, marking campaigns or clients so trends emerge across months and years. This is not busywork. It is a one-time investment that yields years of clarity. The future version of you, hunting for patterns or tax evidence, will be grateful.

The principle echoes across disciplines. Librarians impose catalogues, not to burden readers but to unlock collections. Scientists impose taxonomies, not to complicate knowledge but to make it searchable. Your chart of accounts, naming conventions included, plays the same role. It is your private catalogue, the infrastructure of financial clarity. Without it, numbers scatter into noise. With it, they form a system that speaks.

What makes this subject urgent today is the sheer abundance of financial tools at our fingertips. Bank feeds, invoicing apps, payment processors—they all deliver data at velocity. But without a clear structure to receive and organise it, the flood becomes overwhelming. Many freelancers experience their accounting software as a source of guilt precisely because its default categories feel misaligned. They are working within someone else's mental model. To reverse the relationship—to make the chart of accounts think like *you*—is to reclaim sovereignty over your own numbers.

And the lesson is timeless. From merchants in ancient markets tallying goods under broad headings, to Renaissance traders refining categories of costs and revenues, clarity has always rested on structure. The question is never only *what is the number?* but *what bucket does it belong to?* The buckets we choose decide the stories our numbers tell. Choose poorly, and the story is noise. Choose wisely, and the story is actionable truth.

This chapter is an invitation to design a chart of accounts that strips away friction, reveals the profit line that matters, protects you from distortion, and equips you with conventions that scale. It is an invitation to see categories not as arbitrary slots but as tools of clarity. Fewer buckets, sharper lenses, stronger decisions.

Yet a tension remains. Can you trust simplicity? Can you resist the temptation to mimic corporate complexity, to add categories until clarity buckles? Can you accept that in accounting, as in design, less is often more? The answer will shape not only the cleanliness of your books but the sharpness of your choices. For in the end, your chart of accounts is not just an accounting artefact. It is a mirror of how you think about your business. Will it distort—or will it reflect, cleanly, what is truly there?

Designing Buckets You Will Actually Use

A graphic designer I once interviewed admitted she had thirty-seven categories in her accounting software. "Meals and Entertainment," "Office Supplies," "Computer Equipment," "Miscellaneous Expenses," "Professional Services," "Subscriptions," and so on. Each time she bought a font licence or paid for a new sketching tablet, she hesitated. Was it software? Equipment? Subscriptions? By the end of the year, her reports were a patchwork of inconsistencies. She had been meticulous, yet the numbers told her nothing clear. Despite hours spent classifying, she could not answer a simple question: *How much did I really make after delivering the work?*

This is the paradox of traditional accounting structures. More categories feel like precision, but in practice they breed hesitation and error. A one-person business is not a corporation; it does not need the labyrinthine detail designed for shareholders and auditors. What it needs is speed, accuracy, and clarity—numbers that can be trusted quickly enough to guide decisions. The irony is that the simplest structure often produces the cleanest insights. Fewer buckets do not mean less understanding. They mean more.

At its core, every business—whether a multinational or a solo freelancer—performs three functions: earning, delivering, and running. Money flows in because of earning. Costs are incurred while delivering. And running is everything else that keeps the lights on. By aligning categories to these three natural rhythms, every transaction finds a "default destination." A client invoice falls into earning. A subcontractor's fee belongs in delivering. A Zoom subscription sits in running. The friction vanishes. You no longer deliberate with every line item; you drop it into the stream it naturally belongs to.

Why does this matter so much? Because categorisation is not a clerical chore. It is the foundation of clarity. A messy structure distorts your view of profitability, misguides your pricing, and wastes precious mental energy. A clean one accelerates both trust and action. Consider the difference between two reports: one that scatters software expenses across five overlapping categories, and another that simply shows whether software supports delivery or running. The first leaves you second-guessing. The second instantly tells you whether those tools are helping you earn more than they cost.

The concept of default destinations deserves emphasis. When every transaction already has a natural home, bookkeeping stops feeling like a quiz. A web host subscription always goes to "running." Payment to a freelance illustrator always goes to "delivering." The consistency builds over time until your reports become not just tidy but trustworthy. What you see is what you can act on.

Philosophically, this echoes a deeper truth about human decision-making. We falter when choices are open-ended. The energy wasted debating minor distinctions erodes our capacity to think about what matters. Structure is liberating, not constraining. A small set of buckets is like a well-marked map: it narrows ambiguity and accelerates movement. And in a one-person business, where attention is scarce, that liberation is priceless.

Consider a consultant who once divided expenses into twenty-one categories, mirroring the chart of accounts he found in a corporate template. Each month, he spent two hours classifying, often guessing when items overlapped. When he rebuilt his system around just three streams—earning, delivering, running—his weekly close shrank to thirty minutes. More importantly, he finally saw that "delivering" costs were consuming nearly half his revenue, largely due to subcontractors. Armed with this clarity, he renegotiated contracts and raised project fees. Within a year, his profit margin had doubled. The fewer buckets revealed the line that mattered.

This is not just about efficiency; it is about honesty. Too many categories tempt you to hide uncomfortable truths. You may bury personal expenses under "miscellaneous" or scatter delivery costs into general overhead, flattering your margins. With three streams, there is nowhere to hide. If delivering eats most of your income, the report shows it plainly. If running costs are ballooning, the excess is obvious. Simplicity enforces accountability.

The contrast with corporate accounting is stark. Large firms have armies of analysts to interpret dense charts of accounts. A solo operator has only themselves. The elegant solution is not to replicate corporate structures but to design one fit for scale of one. Instead of drowning in categories, you strip down to what directly informs decisions. Fewer buckets mean fewer chances to distort reality, whether by accident or by habit.

There is also a psychological shift. When categories feel aligned to the way you actually think, bookkeeping ceases to be alien. It becomes almost conversational. You earn, you deliver, you run. The language is human, not bureaucratic. This resonance matters because finance is not just about compliance; it is about relationship—your relationship with your numbers. When the system speaks your language, you listen more closely.

Yet a subtle tension remains. Many feel uneasy with so few categories. They worry that they are oversimplifying, that they will miss something important. This anxiety is cultural. We have been taught that detail equals professionalism, that more boxes checked means better stewardship. But what counts in a one-person business is not ornamental precision; it is actionable clarity. The test is simple: does this structure help you decide faster, with greater confidence? If yes, then it is the right structure.

Designing buckets you will actually use is, in the end, an act of self-respect. It acknowledges that your time is too valuable to be squandered on needless categorisation, that your energy should be directed toward creating value, not wrestling with categories. It is not about rejecting complexity for its own sake, but about refusing unnecessary friction.

So the question lingers: will you embrace the simplicity that reveals, or cling to the complexity that conceals? The answer will not only shape the neatness of your books but the sharpness of your decisions. For every transaction tells a story, and the buckets you design decide whether that story is muddled or clear.

Direct vs Indirect Costs—The Profit Line That Matters

A freelance web developer once told me she thought she was making a solid living. Projects came in steadily, her invoices were being paid, and her revenue line looked healthy. Yet at the end of the year she had little left to show. She blamed high taxes and unpredictable clients—until she reclassified her books. What she discovered was sobering: most of her "overhead" costs were, in fact, directly tied to delivering client work. Subcontractor fees, specialist plug-ins, even certain software licences—all were essential to completing projects but had been buried in general expenses. Once she separated these as *direct costs*, her contribution margin—the amount left after covering the true cost of delivering—was far slimmer than she believed. The business wasn't broken. Her pricing was.

This illustrates the critical line that too many one-person businesses miss. Revenue, on its own, is seductive but incomplete. The line that matters is the one that sits between direct costs and everything else: contribution margin. It is the truest measure of whether the work you do is *worth doing*. And the accuracy of that line depends entirely on one thing—classifying costs correctly.

Misclassification is more common than error. It comes from habit, or from software defaults that were designed for corporate accounting rather than solo operators. A video editor might list freelance animators under "Professional Services" in overhead when, in reality, they are direct costs tied to project delivery. A coach might categorise Zoom as a general subscription, ignoring that for her, it is a direct delivery tool. These small missteps add up to a distorted picture. The books may look clean, but the story they tell is false.

Why does this distinction matter so deeply? Because contribution margin is not just an accounting technicality. It is the pivot of strategy. It tells you which projects, packages, or clients are genuinely profitable. If you bury subcontractor fees or delivery software under overhead, your contribution margin inflates artificially. You may think a project earns you £3,000 after costs, when in truth, £1,500 went out the door to deliver it. The difference is not trivial. It is the difference between repeating a profitable project and sleepwalking into slow financial erosion.

Clarity here anchors pricing decisions. If you see that a project consistently leaves only 20 per cent margin after direct costs, you face a choice: raise the price, reduce delivery costs, or stop offering it. Without this clarity, you might celebrate revenue milestones that are hollow victories. A £100,000 turnover sounds impressive until you discover that £70,000 went into delivering it, leaving you less resilient than a peer who earned £60,000 with a leaner cost base.

The task, then, is to sort costs into two distinct families. Direct costs—sometimes called cost of sales—are those without which you cannot deliver the service or product. Indirect costs, or overhead, keep the business running but are not tied to any specific project. The distinction is intuitive once you see it, yet subtle in practice. A subscription to Adobe Creative Cloud, for example, may be a direct cost for a graphic designer but an overhead for a consultant who uses it occasionally for formatting slides. The same line item can sit in different places depending on its role.

A practical way to cut through ambiguity is the "if-this-client" test. Ask: *If I did not have this client or project, would I still incur this cost?* If the answer is no, it is direct. If yes, it is indirect. Subcontractor hours, project-specific plug-ins, printing for a client report—all vanish when the project vanishes. Rent, insurance, broadband, and general marketing do not. This test strips away grey areas, grounding classification in lived reality rather than theory.

History offers a reminder of why this clarity matters. In the early industrial age, manufacturers tracked their raw materials and labour meticulously because they knew these dictated survival. Only later, with the growth of managerial bureaucracy, did overhead swell into sprawling charts that obscured the profit line. For the solo business, the lesson is not to reject overhead but to resist letting it swallow direct costs. Precision at this line is not a luxury; it is the foundation of self-preservation.

Modern case studies reinforce the point. A freelance photographer discovered that assistant fees and equipment rentals, long buried in "Miscellaneous Expenses," consistently ate 40 per cent of her project fees. When she separated them as direct costs, she realised her day rates were unsustainably low. Within six months of repricing, she doubled her retained profit without working longer hours. Similarly, a coach who split Zoom and transcription software into direct costs recognised that his group programme margins were far stronger than his one-to-one sessions. He shifted focus accordingly. Neither change required growth. Both required clarity.

The philosophical dimension is equally important. Where you draw the line between direct and indirect costs reflects how honestly you want to see your business. It is tempting to bury uncomfortable expenses in overhead, keeping contribution margin artificially rosy. But self-deception here is dangerous. It postpones hard decisions, encourages underpricing, and breeds fragile strategies. The courage to face the true line—however lean it looks—is the beginning of real control.

And yet, a lingering question remains. How simple should the separation be? Too much granularity and the system collapses under its own weight; too little and you risk obscuring truths. The balance lies in disciplined categorisation supported by a simple worksheet. Take the list of all your expenses and run the "if-this-client" test. Move the grey items deliberately. Re-run your P&L with the new classifications. The exercise may take an hour, but its impact will echo for years.

Contribution margin is not just an accounting measure. It is the story of whether your work sustains you. It is the line that tells you when a project is fuelling your business and when it is quietly draining it. Yet it is also a fragile line, vulnerable to distortion if you do not draw it carefully. Every decision downstream—pricing, strategy, even what kind of work you say yes to—rests upon its accuracy.

So the challenge is clear. Will you classify with courage, accepting that some projects you cherish may look less profitable than you hoped? Will you face the discomfort of reclassifying and confronting the truth? Or will you continue to let overhead blur the line, enjoying the comfort of inflated margins while silently eroding your base? The numbers will not lie. But whether you choose to see them honestly is a decision only you can make.

Personal vs Business—Guardrails, Not Guilt

A photographer once confessed that the most stressful part of her business wasn't clients, deadlines, or even taxes—it was her bank account. Every time she bought groceries, her business card was closer to hand than her personal one. Every time she paid for new equipment, she debated whether to use the household account or the business one. By year's end, the two streams were tangled. Her accountant estimated her tax liability based on numbers inflated by personal expenses. When the actual calculation came back, she owed far more than she had set aside. The problem wasn't dishonesty. It was commingling. And it nearly broke her.

This is where many one-person businesses falter. The challenge is not the complexity of accounting rules but the blurred lines of everyday life. When you *are* the business, your wallet is both personal and professional. A coffee can be both sustenance and a client expense. Your laptop is both a Netflix machine and the tool that earns your living. The overlap is real. What matters is not striving for an impossible perfection in separation, but establishing guardrails—practical boundaries that prevent errors from compounding and stop anxiety from festering.

The paradox is that guilt drives more financial chaos than negligence. Many solo operators torment themselves over minor mistakes—forgetting to separate a meal, accidentally charging a personal subscription to the business card. The shame feeds procrastination, and procrastination breeds disorder. A better frame is not guilt but guardrails: pragmatic structures that reduce errors automatically, while allowing for imperfection. You are not trying to satisfy an auditor's fantasy of tidiness. You are trying to protect your cash, your attention, and your peace of mind.

The most powerful guardrail is deceptively simple: two accounts. One for business, one for personal. This single division, more than any spreadsheet or software, transforms clarity. When all income lands in the business account, and all expenses related to earning and delivering flow out of it, you have already eliminated 80 per cent of confusion. The personal account then becomes a sanctuary, holding what is safe to spend as household money. This structure does not prevent every error—there will still be moments of crossover—but it makes errors visible and manageable.

Paired with the two-account rule is another: one capture inbox. All receipts, invoices, and statements—whether digital or physical—should flow into a single channel. It could be a folder in your cloud storage, an accounting app, or even a dedicated email address. The key is that everything has a default home, a place you can trust to contain the paper trail. Without this, documents scatter: one in your downloads folder, another in your glove box, a third lost in an email thread. Scatter breeds oversight; centralisation breeds calm.

The benefits are not only organisational but psychological. With guardrails in place, the fear of "missing something" recedes. You no longer need to hover over every expense with suspicion. You trust the structure to catch errors, and you trust yourself to correct them in weekly or monthly reviews. Anxiety lessens not because mistakes disappear but because mistakes lose their sting.

The case for separation grows stronger when viewed through tax. Consider the freelance illustrator who mingled business and personal expenses on the same card. She estimated her tax based on a rough tally of income and outgoings. But because personal expenses were buried in the mix, her books understated profit. She set aside too little, assuming she had earned less than she actually had. The result was a painful tax bill and a drained savings account. Had she run her transactions through separate accounts, her estimates would have been truer, and the shock avoided. Commingling does not just cloud clarity—it distorts reality in ways that compound over time.

The counterpoint is obvious: life is messy. Few people want to carry two wallets everywhere, or pause at every purchase to consider which account to use. The answer is not rigidity but tolerance. A small number of misallocations are inevitable. What matters is that the system catches them. During your weekly or monthly close, you reassign misfiled items to their rightful side. The aim is not a flawless record in real time, but an honest record in the cycle that matters. Perfectionism paralyses; pragmatism liberates.

There is also a deeper philosophical current running beneath this practice. Boundaries are the architecture of trust. Just as clear working hours separate labour from leisure, and contracts separate expectations from assumptions, financial guardrails separate the personal self from the professional entity. Without boundaries, everything blurs: your savings, your security, your sense of self-worth. Money becomes a fog. With boundaries, you see clearly what is yours, what belongs to the business, and how the two can sustain one another without sabotage.

Yet we should resist the fantasy that guardrails erase all tension. The temptation to blur lines will return: a personal trip partially justified as a research expense, a family purchase made on the business card in the rush of the day. These are not signs of failure; they are the lived reality of small business. The measure of maturity is not the absence of mistakes, but the discipline of correction. Guardrails exist not to keep you perfect, but to keep you safe.

So the choice is stark but liberating. Will you continue to carry the low-grade anxiety of muddled accounts, forever unsure whether you are overspending, under-saving, or mis-estimating? Or will you install simple, forgiving boundaries—two accounts, one inbox—that make clarity the default rather than the exception? The first path promises guilt and guesswork. The second offers calm, not by removing complexity but by containing it.

And yet a question lingers: can you trust yourself enough to let the guardrails do their work? Or will you cling to guilt, mistaking it for rigour? The difference will shape not only your tax bill but your peace of mind. For in the end, separating personal from business is not about compliance. It is about reclaiming attention, protecting cash, and living without the constant hum of financial doubt.

Naming Conventions and Codes That Scale

One of the great paradoxes of small business finance is that the smallest decisions—how you type a vendor's name, whether you tag a transaction with a client code, what you write in the memo field—shape the speed and clarity of your books more than almost any software feature. A single inconsistency multiplies into chaos. "Google Cloud," "Google," and "GCP" become three different line items. A marketing campaign filed under "Autumn Ads," "Fall push," and "October launch" prevents quick comparison. When the time comes to ask, *Which client is actually profitable?* or *Which campaign brought the highest return?* the answers are buried in noise of our own making.

The irony is that most founders believe they have a data problem when in fact they have a language problem. Data is only as good as the words that frame it. If names are inconsistent, categories unstable, and codes absent, no dashboard can deliver clarity. Search queries fail, patterns vanish, and the supposedly objective ledger becomes a hall of mirrors. Yet with a handful of disciplined conventions—consistent vendor names, lightweight client and campaign codes, and concise memo tags—the same ledger becomes a living map, a source of truth you can interrogate in seconds. Implement it once, and the benefits compound for years.

The lesson is hardly new. Medieval scribes, tasked with maintaining accounts for abbeys and merchants, relied on carefully standardised scripts to ensure ledgers could be read across generations. A slanted "s" or a double loop might change the interpretation of an entire page. In commerce, precision of naming has always been the hinge of continuity. What differs today is not the principle but the scale: in a digital system, a misnamed entry does not merely confuse one clerk—it fractures every future query. Consistency is leverage.

Take the case of a solo consultant running client projects across three industries. In the first year, she logged software subscriptions as "Zoom," "Zoom Video," and "Zoom.us," depending on the billing statement. When she attempted to calculate her communications costs across projects, the export showed three separate vendors. Only by manually reconciling them did she realise the tool consumed a larger slice of her margin than expected. A year later, she imposed a convention: all subscriptions would be logged with the vendor's full legal name as it appeared in the invoice header, no exceptions. Overnight, her exports became trustworthy. Decisions that once took hours of reconciliation could be made in minutes.

But naming alone is not enough. Memo tags and lightweight codes bring the ledger to life. Imagine recording every client payment with a two- or three-letter code—RIV for Riverstone, ARC for Arcadia—paired with a simple memo such as "Q2 retainer" or "Launch project fees." A year later, you want to know whether Riverstone retainers or Arcadia project launches generated higher cash flow volatility. With coded memos, the query takes seconds. Without them, you scroll through rows of near-identical entries, hoping to reconstruct intent from half-forgotten context.

The sceptic may ask whether such discipline is worth the friction. Isn't the point of modern accounting software that it automates categorisation? Yes and no. Automation accelerates inputs, but only on the terms you give it. A bank feed that sees "Amazon" will categorise it as "Office Supplies" regardless of whether the expense was a client gift, a server fee, or a last-minute microphone for a presentation. Without conventions and codes, the automation misleads. With them, it magnifies your clarity.

This is where philosophy meets pragmatism. The essence of a system that scales is not complexity but repeatability. If your naming conventions are elaborate, they collapse under real-world pressure. If they are simple but unyielding—*always full vendor name, always client code, always memo tag*—they become habits as natural as fastening a seatbelt. The aim is not bureaucratic tidiness but velocity. Each choice you standardise today is one fewer decision tomorrow, one less moment of hesitation when the stakes are high.

Consider the case of a creative agency that introduced campaign codes to track marketing spend. Before codes, their quarterly review was an exercise in guesswork. Was the "Spring push" the same as "April ads"? Did "Q2 promo" overlap with "Summer launch"? Arguments flared. After introducing three-character codes assigned at project inception, they could compare campaigns across time with a single filter. Within two quarters, they discovered that a campaign type they had assumed was unprofitable was in fact their highest-yielding once mislabelled entries were corrected. The codes did not change reality. They revealed it.

There is an intellectual elegance in this: clarity emerges not from adding more data but from tightening the frame through which data is seen. The historian depends on chronology; the scientist on measurement units; the small business on naming conventions. Each is a grammar of order, a way of making chaos tractable. And, like grammar, once learned it disappears into fluency. No one marvels at subject–verb agreement, but without it, communication collapses. Likewise, no one celebrates a correctly tagged vendor, but without it, decisions drift into vagueness.

The true cost of neglect is not the time lost in reconciliation but the opportunities missed. A mislabelled subscription hides recurring bloat. An inconsistent client name prevents analysis of lifetime value. A vague memo field erases the evidence you will need to adjust pricing or renegotiate terms. These are not clerical inconveniences. They are strategic blindfolds. The margin for a solo operator is often thin. To missee it is to mismanage it.

And yet, perfection is not required. The aim is not to police every keystroke but to institutionalise a shared language between you and your future self. You are building a ledger that you can interrogate in six months, twelve months, five years, without relying on memory. You are creating the ability to ask: *Which clients reward me most reliably? Which vendors creep in costliest? Which campaigns deserve another run?* Without naming conventions and codes, these questions remain frustratingly rhetorical. With them, they become answerable.

The deeper question lingers: if consistency is so powerful, why do so few adopt it? The answer may be psychological. Humans tolerate ambiguity better than discipline in the short term. It is easier to type "Amazon" and move on than to pause, tag, and code. But every shortcut is a debt, and debts always come due. The reckoning arrives at tax season, in a cash flow crunch, or during a strategy review where clarity is needed most. Guardrails, once again, prove less restrictive than they appear.

So the challenge for any one-person business is not whether to adopt naming conventions and codes but whether to accept the cost of not doing so. Will you continue to live with exports that deceive and dashboards that confuse? Or will you invest a sliver of discipline today in exchange for years of reliable clarity? The ledger is always speaking. The only question is whether you have taught it a language you can understand.

Chapter 3
The Weekly Close: 45 Minutes to Calm

On Sunday evenings, in a quiet flat above a bustling London high street, a graphic designer closes her laptop and slips a leather pouch onto the kitchen table. Inside is nothing more exotic than a notebook, a pen, and a login card for her banking app. She makes a pot of tea, silences her phone, and begins. For forty-five minutes she sits not as a harried freelancer but as the chief steward of her own business. By the time she stands, her numbers are tidy, three decisions are noted for the week ahead, and the quiet satisfaction of order has replaced the dull ache of avoidance. Monday will not arrive as a surprise; it will arrive as a plan.

The paradox is that finance, the domain so many treat as a reactive scramble, becomes most powerful when approached as ritual. A ledger is not tamed by intensity but by cadence. The weekly close is not an act of paperwork; it is a standing appointment with yourself in which money ceases to be a source of vague unease and becomes a source of specific insight. Those who establish this rhythm discover that numbers stop shouting in crises and begin whispering early warnings, if only you're willing to sit still long enough to listen.

History is full of parallels. Medieval merchants of the Hanseatic League recorded their trading accounts on a fixed cycle, closing books each week to ensure partners scattered across ports could be held accountable. In modern hospitals, surgical checklists are repeated with disciplined regularity, not because the surgeons forget the steps but because ritual protects attention in environments prone to error. The same is true for the solo business. You do not build resilience by waiting for disaster; you build it by setting aside a predictable time, however brief, to sweep the floor, tighten the bolts, and re-anchor yourself in reality.

The weekly close works because it transforms finance from a lurking shadow into a compact habit. Rather than one monumental, exhausting "catch-up" at year-end, you touch the system lightly but consistently. Every transaction has a home. Every invoice is either cleared or consciously noted. Every week ends with the ledger caught up to the present, so nothing ferments into guilt or confusion. The entire process is bounded by a timer—forty-five minutes, no more. It is the difference between a daily toothbrushing routine and the dread of an emergency root canal: regular, ordinary, preventive.

The heart of this chapter is not technical but psychological. Most small operators know, in principle, that they ought to check their accounts more regularly. What they lack is not information but a frame. The weekly close provides that frame, breaking the work into four tightly defined movements: prepare the surface, capture and clear the inbox, categorise with rules, and compare to decide. Each is narrow enough to be finishable yet meaningful enough to matter. Once these movements are named, you can notice which one falters, fix it quickly, and restore the loop. It is finance reduced to its essence.

There is also a moral subtlety to this ritual. Numbers can feel adversarial—an arena of mistakes, forgotten receipts, unfiled statements. The weekly close repositions them as an act of care. To sit with your accounts once a week is to acknowledge that your work deserves stewardship, that your future self deserves clarity. It is not punishment, and it is not penance. It is self-respect in ledger form. Many discover that, after a few weeks, what once felt like drudgery begins to feel like a strangely calming conversation with oneself.

The consequences ripple outward. A designer who clears her transaction inbox weekly finds that she never faces a pile of half-sorted statements come tax season. A coach who writes down three micro-decisions each week—*stop one spend, check one price, chase one invoice*—finds, six months later, that her pricing has sharpened, her costs have slimmed, and her receivables are under control. These are not heroic interventions but tiny disciplines compounded. The ledger ceases to be an archive of what happened and becomes a rehearsal for what will happen next.

And yet, the test is not whether you can perform a perfect close every week, but whether you can maintain the rhythm when tired, distracted, or pressed. Ritual succeeds where willpower fails. The close works precisely because it is designed to be small, bounded, and repeatable. Set the environment—same time, same tools, same tea or playlist—and the mind falls into its groove. You are no longer negotiating with yourself about whether to "do the books." You are simply keeping an appointment.

The deeper question is this: what would your business feel like if your financial reality never ran more than seven days out of date? If every Monday you began not with uncertainty but with three crisp priorities shaped by evidence? That is the promise of the weekly close. Not perfection, not even ambition, but calm. A rhythm that returns your attention to where it belongs: the work itself, the clients you serve, the life you are building. Numbers handled, quietly and quickly, then put back in their place.

What follows is not another method to add to your burden but a small design for freedom: a loop you can finish in under an hour, every week, that dissolves anxiety before it grows. The question is not whether the ritual works. It is whether you are willing to give yourself the gift of calm by making it real.

Prepare the Surface

There is a reason why monks sweep temple courtyards before prayer. The act is not primarily about dust but about attention. To clear the surface is to prepare the mind. In the same way, approaching your numbers without preparing the ground is like attempting to read by candlelight in a gale. The flame flickers, the pages blur, and what might have been a moment of clarity becomes one of strain. The weekly close begins not with figures but with environment. It is an act of preparation, of setting the stage so that finance is no longer a fight against distraction but a quiet conversation with yourself.

Most small business owners do not fail at bookkeeping because they lack intelligence. They fail because they treat the work as an afterthought, snatched in odd moments between emails or late at night when energy is thin. Numbers tackled in that state become adversaries. Each transaction feels like a rebuke, each report like a reminder of what was neglected. By contrast, when the work is framed as a ritual, its meaning changes. A cleared desk, a fixed time, a simple kit of tools—these are signals to the brain that what follows is not a chore but a deliberate practice. Psychology research on "implementation intentions" shows that behaviour becomes far more consistent when it is anchored to a time and place. If your ledger has an appointment on Tuesday at four o'clock, with a pot of tea and a checklist, procrastination has fewer places to hide.

Consider the designer who, after months of avoidance, set a recurring calendar hold for her weekly close. She gathered her laptop, a bank card reader, and a folder marked "inbox" into a small box. The kit lived on a shelf by her desk. Every Friday at 9 a.m. she opened the box, cleared her transactions, and closed it again. The box became a ritual object. The act of opening and closing was as important as the work itself: it bounded the task, made it finite, and signalled completion. The result was not only cleaner books but a sense of calm that spilled into other areas of her business. The ritual had reframed her relationship with finance from avoidance to stewardship.

There is a deeper lesson here. Environments are not neutral. The context in which you approach your accounts will shape the quality of your attention. A cluttered desk invites wandering thoughts. A buzzing phone fractures focus. Even small frictions—searching for a missing password, hunting for a statement—can sap the limited willpower you bring to the task. Preparing the surface means stripping away these frictions in advance, so that your finite energy is spent on decisions rather than on logistics. A no-distraction checklist—phone silent, notifications off, documents to hand—seems mundane, yet it is the scaffolding on which reliable routines are built.

This is why the weekly close should be treated less as an errand and more as a standing meeting with yourself. When you schedule meetings with clients, you protect the time, prepare the materials, and show up on time. Why should your own business deserve less? Framing the close as an internal appointment signals respect—for your work, for your future self, and for the financial truth that underpins your choices. It also subtly raises the stakes. Skipping a meeting with yourself feels less trivial than "putting off the books."

You become both the chair and the attendee, accountable to your own calendar.

The act of preparation also reframes numbers emotionally. Too many treat financial reviews as punitive: a moment when reality delivers its verdict. But when the ritual is set with care—a chosen playlist, a tidy surface, a fresh notebook—the numbers are softened. They cease to be a judgment and become information. Just as a doctor reviews test results not with dread but with clinical curiosity, so the business owner can learn to sit with their accounts as evidence, not accusation. A prepared surface turns finance from guilt into guidance.

One might argue that such rituals are a luxury, a distraction from the "real work" of selling and delivering. But history suggests otherwise. From the ledgers of Venetian merchants to the logbooks of polar expeditions, disciplined record-keeping has always been paired with ritual preparation. The explorers who survived were those who treated daily log entries as non-negotiable, even when storms raged. They knew that order on paper was a form of survival. In our era, the storm is not ice but information. Ritual is the anchor.

The practicalities are simple, though the impact is profound. Choose a recurring time and protect it. Assemble a "close kit" with everything needed—laptop, login credentials, checklist, capture folder—so the start is frictionless. Clear your workspace, silence distractions, and mark the ritual with a small sensory cue: a cup of coffee, a lamp switched on, a piece of music. These cues are not decoration; they are triggers that shift the brain into the right mode. When repeated weekly, they build a groove deeper than willpower.

The paradox is that the more you invest in preparation, the less energy the work itself requires. Numbers reviewed in distraction demand twice the effort and yield half the insight. Numbers approached in ritual flow more easily, because attention is unbroken. Over weeks, this discipline compounds. Patterns emerge sooner, decisions are made with confidence, and the anxiety that once clung to finance begins to recede. You stop wrestling with numbers and begin conversing with them.

But the unresolved question remains: if preparation is so simple, why do so few do it? Perhaps because it feels indulgent to create ceremony around money. Perhaps because we imagine discipline must always be grim. Yet the truth is that ritual is the shortest path to freedom. To prepare the surface is not to waste time; it is to invest in clarity. The only question is whether you are willing to slow down for five minutes in order to see the truth that might change your next five years.

Capture and Clear the Inbox

Every business owner has faced it: the creeping dread of a cluttered inbox, not of emails but of money. Bank feeds, PayPal notifications, Stripe settlements, credit card charges, and stray receipts trickle in daily until they pile into a shapeless mound. Left unchecked, that mound becomes something far heavier than numbers—it becomes anxiety. And yet, the paradox is stark: transactions themselves are neutral, often small and unremarkable, but our avoidance magnifies them into looming obstacles. A single taxi receipt or card charge, once delayed, seems to carry an emotional weight out of all proportion. The inbox becomes less a record of business and more a quiet gallery of neglected tasks.

The discipline of capturing and clearing changes this dynamic entirely. Imagine every inflow and outflow—no matter the platform—flowing into one single, central inbox. It becomes the financial equivalent of sweeping the floor each evening: nothing is lost, nothing is hidden under furniture, nothing festers. Order is not created by handling everything at once, but by knowing there is one trusted place where every item waits for attention. Once captured, the act of clearing that inbox becomes not a mountain but a manageable hill, climbed weekly with confidence rather than avoided with guilt.

Here the "one-touch rule" is pivotal. Each transaction is either dealt with immediately—categorised, logged, or attached to a receipt—or it is flagged with a deliberate note for later. What is not permitted is the limbo of "I'll decide later" with no record of why. Every re-handling of a transaction is an invisible tax on your attention. Research into cognitive switching shows that even minor re-exposure drains energy disproportionately: the same line item reviewed three times does not take three times the effort, it takes tenfold in attention, because each return carries the added burden of remembering where you left off. The one-touch rule protects you from this quiet leak of willpower.

Consider a case from a freelance marketing consultant who processed her transactions only sporadically. Each month she would spend hours re-opening browser tabs, hunting through card statements, and guessing at forgotten expenses. A simple payment to a cloud software provider might be re-read four or five times before it was finally filed, wasting time and fraying patience. When she adopted a weekly capture-and-clear ritual with the one-touch principle, her workload halved within a month. More importantly, her attitude changed. The inbox emptied each Friday; she ended the week with closure rather than a list of vague financial ghosts waiting to ambush her later.

The principle is not simply mechanical; it is philosophical. Clearing an inbox is a small rehearsal in trust. You are teaching yourself that no transaction, however trivial, will be abandoned or forgotten. In a sense, you are building a covenant with your future self: when you return to these numbers next week or next month, you will encounter clarity, not chaos. This has profound psychological effects. Studies on "open loops" show that incomplete tasks weigh disproportionately on the mind, draining cognitive bandwidth until they are resolved. By emptying the inbox weekly, you are closing loops, reclaiming attention for creative and strategic work rather than letting it be squandered on background unease.

The process also reframes avoidance. Many small operators secretly believe they will save time by postponing transaction management, yet the opposite is true. Avoidance is compound interest in reverse: the longer you leave it, the more painful it becomes. Clearing, by contrast, creates momentum. Each categorised expense, each logged payment is a small victory, and victories accumulate. The weekly empty inbox becomes not merely a technical outcome but a symbolic one: the business is not drifting, it is being actively steered.

Technology aids this ritual but cannot replace the discipline. Bank feeds, automation rules, and integrations reduce friction, but they are not substitutes for a human making a decision. The point of capture-and-clear is not to offload thought but to compress it: to confront each transaction once, decide its fate, and move on. Automation can route transactions into the inbox and even suggest categories, but only a deliberate system—anchored in the one-touch rule—ensures that nothing lingers without explanation.

The power of this approach lies not only in the hours saved but in the quality of decisions that follow. A weekly cleared inbox means that your financial picture is never more than a few days old. This timeliness matters. If you wait until quarter-end, an overlooked payment or late invoice can grow into a crisis. If you face it weekly, problems surface while they are still soluble. A missed client payment is flagged while the project is still live, not three months after goodwill has faded. An unnecessary subscription is spotted before it drains a year's worth of fees. Information, when current, is leverage. When stale, it is little more than noise.

There is an aesthetic dimension too. An empty inbox at the end of the week provides the same satisfaction as a clean desk or an emptied sink. It signals that the slate is clear, that attention is no longer divided. For many freelancers, this is the first time they experience money as something under their hand, not hovering above them. The inbox becomes not a source of guilt but a site of closure. Numbers lose their sting when they are confronted in an orderly frame.

And yet the question lingers: why do so many resist this discipline when its benefits are so obvious? Perhaps because clearing feels trivial compared to selling or delivering. Perhaps because we confuse importance with urgency, letting client deadlines eclipse internal order. But what if the true test of professionalism is not how we handle clients in the spotlight, but how we handle ourselves in the quiet moments offstage? An inbox cleared weekly is not simply administration. It is a vote for clarity over chaos, for stewardship over drift.

The ritual does not promise to eliminate complexity, only to contain it. Transactions will always arrive, as inevitable as waves on the shore. The discipline of capture and clear is to let them break once, then recede, rather than letting them swirl endlessly at your ankles. The inbox will fill again by next week. That is not failure but rhythm. The unresolved question, and the one worth carrying forward, is this: will you meet the tide with avoidance, or with the calm assurance of someone who knows the sand will be swept clean again?

Categorise with Rules, Not Memory

There is a telling detail in the history of double-entry bookkeeping. The Venetian merchants who refined the system in the fifteenth century did not rely on recollection to know which transactions belonged where. They built rules, consistent and repeatable, so that every entry had a home and every column a meaning. It was not brilliance that made the system endure for centuries, but the decision to remove memory from the equation. Rules preserved clarity long after the moment had passed. The same principle holds for the modern solo business: the enemy of reliable finance is not ignorance but over-reliance on memory.

Memory is seductive. It whispers that you will *remember later* that the £47 charge at midnight was a software subscription and not a dinner. It insists you will recall which Stripe payout included VAT and which did not. But memory is a fragile servant. Studies in cognitive psychology show that short-term recall begins to decay within hours, and that the effort of trying to retrieve small details drains attention needed for higher-order thinking. Every time you rely on memory in finance, you are gambling with accuracy and exhausting yourself in the process. The paradox is that by trying to keep everything in your head, you diminish the very resource—clear thinking—that makes your business viable.

This is where bank rules and automations transform the picture. Instead of manually tagging every expense or tax, you create a system once, and it acts on your behalf indefinitely. A rule might state: "Any charge from Adobe goes to software subscriptions, tagged with VAT." Another: "Any payment from Client A routes to consulting income." Once embedded, these rules execute silently, reducing weekly clicks by half or more. The act of categorising shifts from memory to mechanism. Instead of endless micro-decisions, you review exceptions. Instead of slogging through repetition, you spot patterns.

A freelance photographer once described how liberating this shift became. Before automations, each bank feed review was a slog: scrolling line by line, remembering which purchases were reimbursable, and tagging them by hand. He dreaded the task so much that he delayed it, compounding the burden. When he finally set rules—equipment to "Cost of Sales," studio rent to "Overheads"—his weekly close dropped from ninety minutes to thirty-five. More importantly, he began to trust the numbers. Reports no longer reflected the vagaries of his memory but the consistency of rules. He could look at profit by project and believe what he saw. That trust reshaped his decisions.

The difference is philosophical as much as practical. When you categorise with memory, you are tying your business to the volatility of mood, fatigue, and distraction. When you categorise with rules, you are building infrastructure. Infrastructure does not ask if you are tired; it simply carries the weight. The Romans did not carry water in buckets each day—they built aqueducts once and benefitted for generations. Rules are the aqueducts of modern bookkeeping. They require effort to design, but once in place, they free your attention for strategy rather than drudgery.

There is, of course, a temptation to overbuild. Some owners create elaborate webs of rules, chasing precision at the cost of clarity. The art lies in balance: a handful of well-designed categories that capture the major flows, not an encyclopaedia of micro-tags that drown you in detail. Remember the principle of signal density—enough granularity to change decisions, no more. A simple rule for recurring software will serve you better than twenty nuanced tags that nobody ever reads.

Automation also changes your relationship with error. When categorisation relies on memory, every mistake feels personal—an accusation of forgetfulness. When it relies on rules, errors become opportunities to refine the system. A wrongly tagged transaction is not a lapse but a signal that the rule needs adjusting. This shift softens the emotional burden. Finance becomes less about blame and more about calibration. The solo operator moves from being a harried clerk to a designer of systems.

The larger point is trust. A system built on memory breeds suspicion—*did I get that right? did I forget something?*—and suspicion erodes confidence in reports. A system built on rules, by contrast, builds cumulative reliability. Each week that the rules fire correctly, your trust deepens. Reports become dependable guides rather than dubious approximations. With trust comes speed: you stop double-checking, stop hesitating, and start making decisions quickly. Speed and accuracy climb together, not at odds.

Yet even as rules reduce labour, they invite a deeper question. If the mechanics of categorisation can be handled with minimal thought, what is the role of the business owner? The answer is attention. Automations handle the ordinary so that you can notice the unusual. A spike in travel costs, a sudden dip in income categories, an anomalous tax treatment—these are signals that demand human judgment. Rules are not about abdicating responsibility; they are about conserving your limited cognitive resources for the choices that truly matter.

So the challenge is not simply technical—setting up rules in banking software or accounting tools. It is conceptual: will you design your finance around human frailty or human strength? Will you lean on the unreliable scaffolding of memory, or will you build rules that honour the scarcity of attention?

The truth is that your business will generate hundreds, perhaps thousands, of transactions a year. You cannot hold them all in your head, and you should not try. What you can hold is a system: a small set of rules that turns chaos into order, week after week. The open question, and the one that shapes your future workload and your peace of mind, is whether you will invest the time to build that system—or keep paying the hidden cost of remembering.

Compare and Decide

There is a peculiar irony in business finance: numbers are only ever as useful as the actions they inspire. A spreadsheet can glow with immaculate formatting, ratios can be precise to two decimal places, and yet if nothing changes—no cost trimmed, no price revisited, no overdue client nudged—the numbers remain inert, little more than decoration. The true power of bookkeeping lies not in the elegance of the records but in the decisions they provoke. And crucially, those decisions need not be grand. In fact, the smallest, most repeatable choices often yield the most enduring results.

Consider the routine of a designer who, each Friday, paused for just fifteen minutes to review her weekly close. She asked herself three questions: *Is there one expense I can stop? One price I should check? One client payment I should chase?* It was an unglamorous ritual—no board meetings, no grand strategy documents. Yet within six months, her profit margin rose by eight points. Not through explosive growth or sudden market luck, but through dozens of micro-decisions: cancelling a redundant software licence, nudging up her hourly rate on projects that consistently ran long, ensuring that late-paying clients no longer slipped through the cracks. The rhythm of comparison followed by action reshaped the trajectory of her business.

Why does such simplicity work? Because comparison grounds choice in evidence. Without it, human judgement drifts. We overestimate the importance of what is vivid and underestimate what is quiet. We anchor on past habits rather than present realities. To *compare* numbers—this month against last, forecast against actual, cost against value—is to cut through bias with a blade of context. It is in these contrasts that signals emerge: a marketing spend that creeps upward without commensurate return, a supplier's fee that subtly rises, a pattern of slow collections that strangles cash flow. Without structured comparison, such shifts remain invisible until they become crises.

Yet comparison alone is insufficient. Too many owners nod at the reports, murmur "interesting," and then return to business as usual. The hinge point is decision. And the smaller the decision, the more likely it is to happen. Research into behavioural economics shows that micro-commitments—actions requiring minimal energy but repeated consistently—compound over time in ways that rival large, sporadic interventions. To stop one spend per week is to prevent the creep of waste. To check one price is to anchor value in reality rather than assumption. To chase one invoice is to protect the lifeblood of cash flow. None of these acts change the world in isolation, but together they accumulate into resilience.

The philosopher Aristotle argued that virtue is cultivated not through grand gestures but through habit—*we are what we repeatedly do.* The same holds for financial judgement. Each weekly comparison and decision sharpens discernment. Over time, the mind learns what healthy numbers look like, where fragility hides, which patterns signal risk. Judgement becomes muscle memory, and confidence grows not from blind optimism but from evidence tested against action.

Of course, there is tension here. The modern entrepreneur is surrounded by dashboards, KPIs, and analytic tools promising predictive insight. The temptation is to expand the decision scope endlessly: to track every metric, compare every ratio, consider every option. But the paradox is that more data often leads to paralysis. What matters is not the breadth of comparison but the discipline of it. A deliberate focus on a handful of contrasts, paired with a commitment to act, is far more potent than sprawling analysis that exhausts without resolution.

There is also the matter of keeping score—not in financial terms alone but in learning. A decision log, however modest, converts weekly choices into an archive of insight. By writing down each micro-decision—a cancelled subscription, a renegotiated rate, an invoice chased—you create a history of reasoning. Patterns reveal themselves: repeated overspends in one category, chronic underpricing in another. The log becomes a mirror, showing not only the state of the business but the evolution of your own judgement. Over time, this record is worth as much as any formal financial statement. It tells the story not just of money, but of decision-making itself.

There is, however, a deeper philosophical layer. To compare and decide is to resist passivity, to insist that numbers are not fate but feedback. It is an act of agency. Every weekly review offers a choice: to accept drift or to intervene, however modestly. The one-person business is particularly vulnerable to drift, because there is no board, no finance committee, no external discipline. But this vulnerability is also an opportunity. A single person, reviewing and acting consistently, can redirect the business with an agility larger organisations can only envy.

The challenge lies not in knowing that decisions matter but in building the courage to make them, repeatedly, in the face of uncertainty. Each micro-decision carries the possibility of being wrong: the subscription you cancel might be useful next month, the price you raise might cost you a client. But the refusal to decide is worse. It cedes control to inertia. The discipline of comparing and deciding each week is not about perfection but about momentum—ensuring that your business is always slightly more aligned, slightly sharper, slightly stronger than it was the week before.

And so the paradox: the most powerful financial discipline is not complex forecasting or advanced analytics, but the quiet ritual of three small choices. Stop one spend. Check one price. Chase one invoice. Repeat, week after week. The question that lingers, and the one that shapes the arc of your enterprise, is whether you will treat numbers as static reports—or as living prompts to act. Which will you choose the next time you sit down with your books: observation or decision?

Chapter 4
Reading a P&L Like a Story

When a novelist sits down to write, the order of sentences matters. A single misplaced clause can tilt meaning, obscure motive, or conceal the truth of a character. Financial statements, though stripped of metaphor, function in much the same way. They are narratives disguised as numbers, and the most misread of them all is the profit and loss account. Too many business owners glance at the top line—revenues, sales, turnover—and declare victory. Yet a book judged only by its opening sentence may hide a tragedy in its final chapter. The first line of the P&L tells you how much came in, but the true line—the gross profit, the contribution after direct costs—reveals the real drama. Two businesses with identical revenues can live opposite stories: one racing towards solvency, the other quietly bleeding out.

Consider the tale of two freelancers, each billing £10,000 in a given month. On paper, their triumph appears equal. Yet one spends £7,500 outsourcing design and software tools, while the other delivers projects largely with her own skill and a streamlined toolkit costing only £2,000. One pockets £2,500 in gross profit, the other £8,000. To celebrate their identical revenues is to misread the plot entirely. The lesson is stark: sales volume without margin is little more than noise. The P&L must be read left to right, as a story that unfolds line by line, revealing who truly holds power in the narrative—the client, the supplier, or the business owner herself.

But stories are not written in moments alone. A single chapter cannot explain the arc of a character; nor can a single month's figures capture the trajectory of a business. The danger is recency bias: reacting to one unusually strong or weak month as though it predicts the future. This is why serious readers of financials turn to rolling-twelve views, where each new month replaces the oldest, and a year's worth of rhythm is laid bare. Suddenly, the panicked dip in March reveals itself as the normal seasonal lull. A subtle rise in expenses, invisible month to month, emerges as a creeping trend. A drift in pricing, previously excused as an outlier, becomes a discernible slope. With this broader lens, panic recedes. Pattern recognition takes its place.

Within these patterns lies another gravity, one less visible but just as binding: expenses. They accumulate quietly, like background characters whose influence is underestimated until the climax. Yet when ranked by effect on profit, they reveal a brutal concentration. A handful of costs—the 20 per cent—account for the majority of outflows. This is expense gravity. It explains why eliminating three redundant tools or renegotiating one major contract can transform profitability more than trimming dozens of minor line items. To read a P&L properly is to weigh these gravitational pulls, to identify which expenses orbit too close and threaten to collapse the business's momentum.

And then comes the most vital turn: from story to strategy. A P&L is not an archive of what has been. It is an agenda for what could be. The skilled reader translates insights into experiments: adjusting price points, rebalancing the mix of services, improving utilisation of time and tools. Each lever maps to a practical action for the next month. The statement ceases to be a post-mortem and becomes a playbook. Progress emerges not through grand revolutions but through compounded adjustments, small experiments layered month upon month, until the business tells a different story altogether.

This chapter invites you to read your profit and loss statement not as a static report but as a narrative, with characters, turning points, and lessons. It asks you to retrain your attention—to celebrate not the volume of revenue but the power of margin; to resist panic at monthly swings and instead see patterns across seasons; to recognise the hidden gravity of expenses; and finally, to treat the P&L as a living script for strategic choice. Numbers, once read this way, cease to intimidate. They become the clearest story you own: the story of how your business earns, spends, and grows. The question is whether you will read passively—or whether you will step into the role of author, shaping the chapters yet to come.

Top Line vs True Line

Picture two shopkeepers on the same high street. Each takes in £50,000 in sales one month. To the passer-by, their success appears identical: tills ringing, customers streaming in, receipts neatly stacking up. Yet step behind the counter and you discover a startling divergence. The first shopkeeper spends £40,000 on suppliers and labour, leaving a £10,000 margin. The second spends only £20,000, leaving £30,000 to cover overhead and profit. Both boast the same *top line*. But one is clinging to survival; the other is building wealth. Identical revenues, opposite realities.

This is the trap of the profit and loss account: the tendency to equate sales with success. The top line seduces with its simplicity, a single bold figure that seems to announce victory. But volume alone does not sustain a business. Power lies further down the page, in gross profit—the *true line*. That figure reveals how much of your effort, your skill, and your ingenuity remains after the costs of delivering your work are stripped away. Celebrate sales without margin and you are cheering noise, not substance. The P&L, read properly, is a discipline in seeing past the applause.

For the one-person business, the danger is amplified. When you are both sales team and delivery arm, the temptation is to conflate busyness with prosperity. A calendar full of client calls and a bank account brimming with incoming payments can conceal razor-thin margins that leave you exhausted and underpaid. Freelancers often discover too late that they have effectively subcontracted themselves at below-market wages, chasing projects that cover costs but not contribution. Gross profit, not revenue, tells you whether you are moving forward or standing still.

To retrain attention, you must read the P&L from left to right. Begin not with sales but with contribution margin: revenues minus the direct costs of earning them. This margin is your fuel, the resource that powers everything else—overheads, taxes, savings, reinvestment. Without it, even impressive turnover collapses under its own weight. Consider the consultant who boasts six figures in billings but outsources research, design, and administration to the tune of 70 per cent of those earnings. Compare them to another consultant who bills less but delivers most work directly and spends sparingly. Their contribution margin may be twice as strong. The first runs harder to stay in place; the second moves forward with ease.

The paradox is that the top line is easier to inflate than the true line is to strengthen. Discounts, underpriced projects, or low-margin services can lift revenue figures quickly but weaken profitability. A photographer may double bookings by slashing rates, only to discover that after travel, editing time, and outsourced printing, the gross profit has shrunk. Another photographer may book half as many shoots at premium pricing, preserving time and extracting more margin. From a revenue perspective, the first looks heroic; from a profit perspective, the second is the clear strategist.

The discipline of focusing on the true line forces a shift in mindset. It demands that you interrogate every sale not just by *what it brings in*, but by *what it leaves behind.* Suddenly, sales become less about bragging rights and more about contribution. Questions sharpen: Is this client worth keeping if their project soaks up resources and leaves crumbs behind? Is this service line sustainable if its costs nearly equal its revenues? By reading contribution first, you re-centre decision-making on what actually builds the business, not what flatters the surface.

History offers cautionary tales. Think of the dot-com boom, when companies celebrated explosive revenue growth while ignoring losses. Billions poured into firms that could sell products for pennies more than they cost to deliver—or in many cases, for less. Sales volume ballooned, but margins withered. When funding dried up, those businesses collapsed, undone by their inability to convert top-line noise into bottom-line strength. The lesson is timeless: numbers must be read not for spectacle, but for substance.

And yet, the psychological pull of the top line endures. Human beings are wired to notice scale. Ten clients feel more impressive than three. A six-figure invoice looks grander than a smaller one. But numbers only matter when weighed against what they cost you—in money, in time, in energy. Gross profit, stark and unembellished, cuts through illusion. It is the metric that humbles vanity and empowers clarity.

The retraining of attention begins with habit. Each time you read your P&L, force your eye past sales and onto margin. Linger there. Ask yourself whether the line is growing, whether it is sufficient to sustain and expand. Over time, the habit reshapes perception. Sales still matter—they are the raw material of the story—but they no longer dominate it. The true line emerges as the protagonist, the thread you follow to make sense of the narrative.

Here lies the discipline and the freedom. To celebrate revenue alone is to read only the headline of your business story. To focus on gross profit is to understand its plot. The question, then, is not how much you sell, but how much you truly keep—and whether the story your P&L is telling is one of growth, or one of illusion.

Patterns Over Months, Not Moments

A single month can feel like the whole truth. One strong sales spike convinces the freelancer that growth has finally arrived; one weak month suggests collapse is looming. The tyranny of the immediate distorts judgement, luring business owners into celebrating too soon or panicking too fast. Yet if you zoom out—if you place that same month within a rolling view of twelve—you discover something subtler and truer. The supposed collapse was just February's lull, recurring each year with remarkable consistency. The sudden surge in July? A seasonal effect, not a permanent elevation. The very same numbers that fuelled anxiety or euphoria in isolation begin, in sequence, to tell a calmer story.

This is the paradox: our instinct is to weigh the present most heavily, but business realities often unfold across seasons, not weeks. Psychologists call it *recency bias*: the disproportionate emphasis we give to what has just happened. It is an ancient survival reflex—last night's storm matters more than last year's drought. But in finance, this bias can be costly. Businesses that chase the signal of a single month risk whiplash: expanding staff after one lucky contract, or slashing expenses after a minor dip. The discipline of the rolling-twelve report works as an antidote, training the eye to seek continuity over coincidence.

Take the example of a design consultant who panicked after a June dip in revenue. In isolation, it seemed catastrophic: her client pipeline had suddenly dried up. But when placed in a rolling-twelve view, the pattern revealed itself—June had been weak three years running, coinciding with industry conference season, when budgets were temporarily diverted. The problem was not her pipeline; it was her perspective. Had she reacted hastily—cutting her marketing spend or lowering prices—she would have eroded margins unnecessarily. Instead, with the broader view, she prepared for the June lull, redirecting her time towards internal projects and training. The "problem" became predictable, and with predictability came calm.

The strength of the rolling-twelve is that it transforms raw data into a narrative. A single column of a spreadsheet tells you what just happened; twelve columns stitched together reveal rhythm. Expenses that creep up invisibly month to month become undeniable when stretched across a year. A subtle decline in average project value, easily rationalised in the short term, hardens into evidence when observed across multiple seasons. By demanding a longer horizon, you replace gut instinct with grounded expectation. Planning stabilises; panic softens into pattern recognition.

Seasonality is not just about retail or tourism. Even in knowledge work, patterns emerge. An academic editor may notice that autumn produces a flood of manuscripts as universities return, while December sinks into silence. A freelance developer may find spring unusually buoyant as companies prepare budgets for the new financial year. Each of these patterns is invisible in the immediacy of month-to-month review but obvious in the rolling-twelve. Once recognised, these rhythms reshape behaviour: cash reserves are built in anticipation of quiet months, pricing is adjusted to reflect seasonal demand, marketing campaigns are timed with precision.

The rolling view also exposes *pricing drift*, a phenomenon so gradual it often escapes notice. A copywriter who charges £800 per project may, over twelve months, watch that average slip to £650 as discounts creep in and scope expands. Month by month, the decline is obscured by small fluctuations; only the longer table reveals the erosion. Here lies the power of perspective: by noticing the drift early, the writer can reset boundaries, renegotiate rates, and re-anchor expectations. Without the rolling-twelve, she risks waking up a year later to find her margins permanently diminished.

Yet there is more than practical advantage at stake. The discipline of looking over twelve months is a philosophical training. It teaches patience in a culture obsessed with immediacy. The world celebrates quick wins and viral spikes, but businesses—especially one-person businesses—rarely thrive on sudden bursts. They are shaped by compounding choices, by recognising which shifts are structural and which are temporary noise. To step back from the month and view the year is to resist the tyranny of the now. It is a way of anchoring judgement in continuity, not volatility.

The calm that follows is not passive resignation but strategic composure. Decisions taken in the light of patterns are not reactionary but deliberate. The business owner who sees seasonality coming does not flail at it; she aligns with it. She learns to store strength in the fat months and invest wisely in the lean ones. She recognises that growth is rarely linear but often cyclical, and that wisdom lies in pacing with those cycles rather than denying them.

Still, the practice is not without tension. How do you balance the discipline of long-term pattern recognition with the need to act swiftly when real problems emerge? How do you avoid using the rolling-twelve as a shield for inaction, dismissing genuine warning signs as mere seasonality? Here lies the challenge: perspective must not become complacency. To see patterns is not to excuse all anomalies. It is to contextualise them, to weigh their meaning with discernment.

The profit and loss account, when viewed across twelve months, becomes less like a static ledger and more like a film reel—frames stitched together into motion, telling a story that is richer than any single image. The choice facing every business owner is whether to live in the flicker of a single frame or to attend to the arc unfolding across them all. And the unresolved question is this: when the next anomalous month arrives—as it inevitably will—will you treat it as crisis, or as one beat in a larger rhythm you have finally learned to hear?

Expense Gravity and the 80/20 of Outflows

Every business owner has experienced the peculiar blindness of small spending. A subscription of £15 here, a service charge of £30 there—numbers that feel negligible in the moment but, when multiplied across months and tools, silently expand into something weighty. The paradox is that we often agonise over one-off discretionary purchases—should I really buy that new laptop?—while ignoring the drip of recurring expenses that, taken together, exert far more gravitational pull on profit. It is the unseen accumulation, not the dramatic indulgence, that most often undermines financial health.

The discipline of mapping expense gravity confronts this blindness directly. It rests on a simple observation: most of the pressure on your outflows comes not from dozens of minor items, but from a concentrated few. The Pareto principle—commonly called the 80/20 rule—applies with striking force to expenses. A handful of categories usually account for the bulk of cash leaving your business. The question is not whether small leaks exist (they always will), but which specific drains exert the heaviest pull on your margins, and how deliberately you respond.

Consider the case of a solo consultant who prided herself on frugality. She refused to spend on coffee meetings, used a decade-old laptop, and scoured her accounts each month for stray £10 subscriptions. Yet when she finally compiled her expenses into a ranked report, she was startled: 65% of her outflows came from just three items—subcontractor fees, one software suite, and rent for a co-working space. Her diligent pruning of small costs had saved her pennies, but the gravitational bodies in her financial universe had remained untouched. By renegotiating contractor terms, switching to a more appropriate software tier, and downsizing office space, she improved her profit margin by more than 20% in a single quarter. What made the difference was not frugality but focus.

This is the essence of expense gravity: recognising that outflows are not flat but weighted, clustered around certain centres of mass. Building an "expense gravity report" is nothing more elaborate than ranking your categories of spending by their effect on profit. The order itself teaches you more than any line-by-line drill. It reveals hierarchy. Some items are fixed stars around which everything else orbits—vital infrastructure costs that cannot be reduced without dismantling the business. Others are malleable planets, open to pruning, renegotiation, or redesign. Distinguishing between the two is the work of discernment, not just arithmetic.

Technology costs, for example, often hide surprising elasticity. Many freelancers accumulate layers of overlapping tools—two project management apps, three design suites, a cluster of cloud storage accounts—because each decision felt rational at the time. In isolation, each subscription is justifiable. In aggregate, they weigh down the P&L. The exercise of ranking reveals not only the weight but also the redundancy. Dropping or consolidating just one or two of these items may yield immediate savings without any meaningful loss of capability. The gravitational load lightens.

Labour costs form another centre of mass, particularly when subcontractors are involved. Misclassification often obscures their true weight. A contractor paid per project might be coded as "miscellaneous" or "software support," masking the fact that this is effectively a direct cost of sales. Once reclassified correctly, the contractor's share of revenue becomes glaringly obvious. The gravity report does not moralise about whether you *should* hire subcontractors—it simply makes their weight undeniable. That clarity allows strategic choices: increase prices to reflect the true cost, reduce reliance on external labour, or find ways to improve utilisation. Without such clarity, the pull continues silently, distorting margins.

What is striking is how quickly elasticity can be regained once the true centres of gravity are identified. A one-hour renegotiation with a vendor can reduce annual outflows by thousands. Cancelling or downgrading a redundant software licence creates an instant uplift in net profit. These are not theoretical tweaks but tangible shifts in financial physics. Where the business once felt heavy, dragged by unseen forces, it becomes lighter, more agile, more able to respond to opportunity.

Philosophically, the practice of expense gravity carries a deeper lesson about attention. We live in a culture conditioned to focus on the visible trivialities rather than the hidden weight. Just as individuals count calories in a snack but ignore the unseen effects of chronic stress on health, business owners track the minor indulgences while the structural costs quietly compound. The act of ranking is, at its core, an act of awareness. It forces you to look squarely at the disproportionate realities of your spending and accept that the gravity you feel is not evenly distributed.

Yet a tension remains. How far should one go in pruning or renegotiating before the business becomes hollow? The cheapest option is not always the wisest. Cutting back on subcontractors may save cash in the short term but lead to exhaustion and reduced capacity. Downgrading tools may reduce costs but compromise quality or efficiency. The practice of expense gravity is not austerity by another name; it is alignment. The aim is not to minimise costs indiscriminately but to ensure that every pound spent pulls its weight, exerting gravitational force towards growth rather than waste.

Imagine standing over your ranked report and asking of each major item: does this expense earn its place in my orbit? If the answer is yes, its weight is justified. If the answer is no—or if you hesitate—it may be time to prune, renegotiate, or redesign. What emerges from this process is not just immediate savings but a sharpened sense of elasticity: the ability to expand profit not by chasing endless new revenue, but by releasing unnecessary mass.

The open question is how often to revisit the pull of gravity. Annually? Quarterly? Monthly? Each cadence reveals new truths, for expenses are never static—they creep, drift, and accumulate. To wait too long is to risk finding yourself once again trapped in the heavy orbit of unnoticed outflows. The discipline of returning to the report is not merely about cost control but about cultivating a habit of perspective: of seeing which forces still serve your direction, and which quietly anchor you to the ground.

From Story to Strategy

The paradox of the profit and loss statement is that it is most often treated as a history book. Neat rows of numbers, neatly boxed months, as if the task were to document what has been, not to influence what comes next. For many small business owners, the P&L is an archive: a document sent to the accountant, a ritual of compliance, filed away once reviewed. Yet its true power lies not in what it records, but in what it can provoke. Read with attention, it is not a museum of transactions but a live script for change.

Consider the restaurateur who, staring at his P&L, noticed that although revenues were steady, margins were slipping. Most would have sighed, blamed inflation, and moved on. Instead, he translated the data into action: he tested a price adjustment on three high-demand dishes, rebalanced his menu mix to favour items with better contribution margins, and experimented with staff scheduling to improve table utilisation. Each lever was mapped to one concrete trial. Within a month, the drift reversed. The P&L had ceased to be an epitaph for lost profit; it had become an agenda for strategy.

This transformation hinges on recognising that every line in a P&L hints at levers—adjustable elements that can be pulled, tested, and refined. Of these, three prove consistently decisive: price, mix, and utilisation. Each represents not a distant financial abstraction but an immediate domain of choice. The discipline is to translate story into strategy by asking: *what small, controlled experiment can I run this month on each lever?* This rhythm of experimentation is what compounds progress.

Price is the most obvious yet most avoided lever. Many fear raising prices will scare customers away, overlooking that demand is rarely as brittle as assumed. A freelance designer, for example, might read in her P&L that revenue per project has flatlined despite rising costs. Rather than lamenting, she tests a modest price increase with one subset of clients. The experiment reveals what she had not dared to believe: not only do clients accept the change, but the higher rate signals confidence, attracting more of the kind of projects she values most. The story of her P&L has thus been rewritten through a single lever, pulled with precision rather than fear.

Mix, the second lever, speaks to the composition of what is sold. A business offering multiple products or services rarely profits equally from each. Yet without looking closely at contribution margin, owners often assume volume equates to value. A consultancy discovered that one category of work, though prestigious, consistently produced razor-thin margins once subcontractor costs were included. By contrast, a more modest service line delivered robust profitability. Reading the P&L as story revealed the imbalance. Their experiment was simple: promote the high-margin service more aggressively for a single quarter. The effect was transformative. Revenue growth slowed slightly, but profit surged. Mix had proven more decisive than scale.

Utilisation, the third lever, captures how efficiently resources are employed. For solo operators, this might mean time; for asset-heavy businesses, it might mean capacity. A training company found its classrooms stood empty two days a week. By experimenting with shorter courses that filled those gaps, it increased output without increasing costs. The P&L reflected not just more revenue, but improved conversion of fixed expenses into productive use. Utilisation had quietly magnified profit without requiring any new client acquisition.

What unites these three levers is that they require translation. The P&L does not announce them directly; it whispers their possibilities through patterns. The work is interpretive. It is here that many stall, paralysed by analysis. Numbers are scrutinised, discussed, even worried over, but no lever is pulled. The business remains trapped in story without strategy. What breaks this paralysis is the practice of mapping each insight to a discrete experiment. No grand transformation is demanded—only one trial per lever, for one month. This lowers the psychological stakes while preserving the compounding effect of action.

The discipline echoes scientific method: hypothesis, test, review. If the price experiment fails, it reveals something valuable about demand elasticity. If the mix experiment falters, it clarifies the role of prestige offerings. If the utilisation experiment disappoints, it signals capacity limits worth respecting. Each outcome, whether labelled success or failure, enriches the story the P&L tells, sharpening strategy over time.

Philosophically, this shift reframes the relationship between narrative and choice. To read a P&L as an archive is to accept the past as final. To read it as agenda is to acknowledge that the story is still being written, line by line, decision by decision. The numbers are not destiny; they are prompts. They ask of the owner: *what lever will you pull next?* In this sense, strategy is less about grand plans than about disciplined responsiveness—small, repeated acts that align tomorrow's numbers with today's intent.

Yet the tension remains: how does one avoid being overwhelmed by the sheer multiplicity of levers a business presents? The answer lies in constraint. Limiting the scope to three experiments—one for price, one for mix, one for utilisation—creates rhythm without chaos. This is not everything-at-once strategy, but deliberate iteration. The P&L becomes less a static document than a dynamic scorecard, tracking the resonance of each adjustment, each note played against the larger score of profitability.

The unresolved challenge is psychological. Can business owners learn to resist both the comfort of inertia and the seduction of overhauls? Can they embrace the modesty of single experiments while trusting in their compounding effect? This tension cannot be solved once and for all; it must be lived, month by month, line by line. The P&L will always tell a story. The open question is whether its readers will let it remain a chronicle of the past—or treat it as an unfinished script, inviting them to write the next act.

Chapter 5
Cash Flow You Can Feel

A profitable business can still run out of money. That contradiction has felled companies larger and older than yours. More than one entrepreneur has celebrated a glowing set of accounts—revenues up, margins healthy—only to find the bank balance sinking below zero. Staff salaries are due, a tax instalment looms, the landlord's invoice sits unpaid. Profit, as it turns out, was not enough. The numbers on paper promised strength; the calendar exposed fragility.

The reason is simple but rarely faced head-on: profit is an opinion, cash is a date. Profit tallies accruals and estimates, spreading income and costs across months to satisfy accountants and regulators. Cash obeys none of these conventions. It arrives—or fails to—on specific days, often later than promised. It leaves—always punctually—when rent, suppliers, or taxes demand. To mistake one for the other is to mistake map for territory. If profit is a narrative, cash is an event. And events, unlike stories, cannot be deferred.

Consider the builder who wins a contract worth six figures. The P&L celebrates; turnover looks glorious. But the payment schedule, hidden in the contract's fine print, releases funds only after milestones are certified. Materials must be bought today, wages must be paid every Friday, while the first tranche of income may not land for six weeks. The builder's books show a healthy profit projection, yet his reality is sleepless nights negotiating overdrafts. It is not profit that feeds payroll. It is cash on hand.

This is why cash flow must be felt, not merely calculated. Dates matter more than totals. A calendar view—showing precisely when money will arrive and when it must leave—makes this truth visceral. The act of plotting inflows and outflows transforms abstraction into urgency. Suddenly, that delayed invoice is not an irritation but the difference between solvency and strain. The discipline of reading cash in time rather than in aggregate reshapes behaviour: invoices are nudged earlier, expenses staggered, tax provisions set aside before they ambush. Overdraft risks fall, not by chance, but by clarity.

Yet the challenge for most small businesses is not constructing elaborate forecasts stretching into distant quarters. Accuracy collapses the further out you look. The antidote is the two-week horizon: a moving 14-day forecast that shows what is expected in, what must go out, and what choices remain flexible. It is short enough to be precise, long enough to avert crunches. This rhythm, updated weekly, becomes a lifeline. Panic gives way to measured adjustment: one reminder email to a client, one delayed discretionary spend, one phone call to reschedule a supplier payment. Small interventions compound into stability.

Still, foresight alone cannot secure resilience. Cash must also be stewarded once it arrives. The simplest, most effective method is to set buffers and buckets. First, decide a target buffer—perhaps one month of expenses—that sits untouchable, a reserve against shocks. Then split every inflow automatically into three buckets: taxes, owner pay, and operating costs. This structure, though deceptively plain, changes everything. The business owner ceases to live in fear of the next tax bill; their personal livelihood no longer hinges on last-minute transfers; operating cash becomes visible and bounded. Predictable pay is not a luxury—it is the psychological foundation for making rational decisions.

And when cash thins—as it inevitably will in the rhythm of business—the response must be principled, not panicked. Too often, scarcity drives desperate pleas to clients or indiscriminate cuts that erode trust. A healthier path is to bridge gaps ethically. Ask for deposits upfront; structure milestone billing; trim scope with clarity and respect. Scripts, prepared in advance, preserve dignity on both sides. The relationship remains intact, even strengthened, because discipline replaces ad hoc pleading. Cash health improves without corroding credibility. Resilience grows not from denial of constraint, but from navigating it with integrity.

The chapter that follows will press this truth home: cash flow is not an accounting footnote but the bloodstream of a business. To manage it is to manage energy, attention, and survival itself. The task is not to build complex models, but to cultivate clarity, rhythm, and principled responses. When cash is understood as lived time, when buffers anchor confidence, when experiments bridge shortfalls with integrity, the numbers cease to be abstract. They become tactile, grounding. And in that grounding, calm replaces fear.

Yet the lingering question shadows every owner: will you learn to feel your cash in time, or only when it is gone? The answer determines not just the shape of your accounts, but the resilience of your enterprise, the steadiness of your mind, and the freedom to act without dread. The P&L may tell your story, but cash flow tells your fate.

Profit Is an Opinion; Cash Is a Date

A retailer opens her quarterly accounts and beams. Sales are strong, margins stable, and the accountants have confirmed a healthy profit. Yet as she scans her bank balance, the smile fades. The payroll run is due tomorrow. The rent debit hits next week. A tax instalment looms on the horizon. The cash in the account is a fraction of what the profit statement suggested. On paper she is thriving; in practice she is scrambling.

This paradox is not rare. It is structural. Profit is built on accruals: estimates, allocations, and accounting rules that spread revenues and costs across periods for consistency. Cash, by contrast, is brutally specific. It lands—or fails to—on exact dates. It exits on schedules that rarely bend. One is a story crafted for analysis; the other is an event that dictates survival. To confuse the two is to mistake a photograph for a live broadcast.

The danger is that profit seduces. It reassures owners and boards that the business is sound, even as cash haemorrhages. A large contract booked in June boosts profit instantly, yet the customer may pay in August. A software licence paid annually depresses profit only fractionally each month, yet the entire fee leaves the bank in one hit. Taxes owed accumulate invisibly until deadlines arrive, demanding real money. Profit whispers comfort; cash dictates reality.

To retrain attention requires rethinking how we "see" money. A profit and loss account presents a flowing narrative, left to right:

income at the top, costs beneath, net result at the bottom. But cash insists on a vertical axis of time. It asks not "what is the total?" but "when, exactly?" A simple calendar view can expose the truth. Line up expected inflows alongside fixed outflows. The sight of a thin week—income delayed while obligations cluster—does more to focus the mind than any abstract margin percentage. The calendar makes timing visceral.

Consider the freelancer juggling multiple clients. On her P&L, the year looks promising: steady retainers, a few chunky project fees, costs low. Yet when the invoices are plotted against her actual expense due dates—rent on the first, utilities mid-month, loan repayments quarterly—she sees the crunch points clearly. The month she pays for annual professional insurance coincides with a client's notorious late payments. That single overlap turns a healthy-looking business into one living on overdraft. The profit number offered no warning. The date did.

This perspective shift is not a call to discard profit—it remains vital for measuring efficiency, value creation, and long-term performance. But profit must be tempered with the calendar discipline of cash. Think of it as the difference between strategy and logistics. Strategy tells you where you are heading; logistics determines whether the supplies arrive on time. An army with sound strategy but no food loses. A business with glowing profit but empty accounts fails just as surely.

The practical discipline begins with mapping. Start with recurring obligations—payroll, rent, debt servicing, tax instalments. These are fixed dates, non-negotiable. Next, layer in discretionary spending and variable costs. Finally, plot expected receipts, anchoring them not to the invoice date but to realistic payment dates based on client behaviour. The resulting calendar is less about precision than about clarity. It surfaces holds, gaps, and choke points where cash may run short despite apparent profitability.

This approach dismantles a dangerous assumption: that profit equals cash. It does not. Profit can be delayed, inflated, or eroded by timing differences invisible to the untrained eye. Cash exposes those illusions. And with exposure comes agency. The owner who sees a looming mismatch can act—chase invoices, stagger payments, or draw on a buffer. The one who does not will drift, surprised again and again by shortfalls. Overdrafts become routine, anxiety habitual.

The distinction also redefines what it means to "plan." Traditional business planning often rests on revenue projections and profit targets. These are useful, but they risk abstraction. A cash calendar, by contrast, insists on immediacy. It asks: do you have the funds to cover the next fortnight's obligations? Do the inflows and outflows balance this quarter, not merely over the year? The granularity disciplines thinking, forcing owners to confront not just *whether* they will be solvent but *when* they may tip into danger.

Philosophically, the contrast reveals a deeper truth about business. Profit is narrative—it smooths and interprets. Cash is experience—unforgiving and immediate. Human beings, too, are prone to this split. We tell stories about our lives—careers progressing, relationships strengthening—while living through messy days of bills, deadlines, and surprises. To navigate both, we must hold story and event in balance. In business, as in life, mistaking narrative for reality is perilous.

And so the discipline becomes not simply technical but psychological. To train oneself to "feel" cash dates is to resist the soothing abstraction of profit. It is to embrace the unglamorous but liberating clarity of timing. The benefit is more than reduced overdraft risk; it is a calmer mind, better decisions, and the ability to steer rather than react.

Still, a tension remains: how to reconcile the broad strokes of profit with the sharp edges of cash? How can an owner hold both perspectives without paralysis or contradiction? The answer lies not in choosing one over the other, but in learning to read profit as opinion and cash as fact. The first tells you whether the business creates value. The second tells you whether you can pay your bills on Tuesday. To ignore either is folly.

The unresolved question lingers, demanding attention: are you running your business by the story your accounts tell, or by the calendar that cash enforces? Those who confuse the two may find themselves profitable and bankrupt in the same breath. Those who distinguish them gain not only solvency but clarity—the rare kind of clarity that turns anxiety into foresight.

The Two-Week Forecast

A single invoice, two days late, can unravel a month. For a solo consultant, it may mean the credit card rolls into interest. For a café, it could leave suppliers unpaid and shelves half-stocked. The paradox is striking: businesses can appear profitable on paper yet feel perpetually fragile in practice because the timing of cash flows, not the magnitude of profit, dictates stability. The antidote to this fragility is not a sprawling annual plan but a tool disarmingly modest in scope—the rolling two-week forecast.

Unlike grand projections stretched across quarters or years, the 14-day window trades ambition for precision. It does not attempt to predict distant futures but to illuminate the immediate horizon where choices and consequences collide. The horizon is short enough to forecast with accuracy, long enough to anticipate crunches before they land. A small design change in perspective—days rather than months—transforms the practice of financial management from abstract speculation into lived strategy. It is not theory; it is triage and foresight combined.

The genius of the two-week forecast lies in its simplicity. It reduces the vast tangle of business finance to three categories: what is expected to come in, what must be paid, and what choices remain. Into the first bucket fall invoices due, transfers from clients, or payments scheduled to arrive. Into the second bucket belong payroll, rent, utilities, debt servicing—non-negotiable obligations. Into the third fall discretionary items: the ad campaign you could delay, the software upgrade you might postpone, the equipment purchase that can wait.

Seen together in a calendar-like view, these three streams create a living map. Patterns surface: the week a retainer lands is secure, but the fortnight that follows looks precarious without nudging a client to pay. The credit card repayment looms just as a project invoice is habitually late. With this view, problems cease to be surprises; they become visible, actionable tensions. The owner can act in advance, nudging an invoice, deferring a choice, or shuffling discretionary spend. Decisions regain their margin of calm.

Consider the case of a small design agency. The partners often found themselves panicking at the end of each month, drawing on personal savings to plug gaps. Their annual accounts showed healthy profit, yet stress never lifted. Only when they began plotting cash on a 14-day rolling view did the truth emerge: a single client, paying irregularly, created predictable troughs every second week. By asking for partial advance payments—a modest adjustment—they transformed a recurring crisis into a manageable rhythm. Profit had not changed; attention had.

Philosophically, the two-week forecast challenges a deep human bias: the tendency to overweight the immediate and neglect the near future. Behavioural economists call it recency bias—the lure of the most recent experience distorting our sense of trend. A single fat invoice received today lulls an owner into false security, while the payroll due in eleven days remains invisible. The two-week window resists this bias. It brings the near future into the present, forcing the mind to see the consequences not of "someday" but of next Friday.

Technology makes this discipline lighter than ever. A spreadsheet with three columns—expected in, must-pay, choices—is enough. Add dates, update weekly, and roll it forward. With practice, the habit takes minutes. Some entrepreneurs build simple automations to pull in invoices and scheduled payments, but the sophistication of the tool matters less than its regularity. The discipline is weekly, not occasional. Its power lies not in perfection of prediction but in the cumulative awareness it builds.

The psychological effect is profound. Owners who once checked their bank balance with dread begin to approach finance as a navigable game. The numbers stop being a source of anxiety and become coordinates on a map. Stress drops because surprises fall. Over time, confidence grows—not the false bravado of endless hustle but the quiet confidence of foresight. The business feels sturdier, not because profit is higher, but because cash is visible.

Yet a tension remains. The two-week forecast is by definition narrow. It cannot replace longer-term planning; it cannot model strategy. It is a tactical tool, not a vision. But therein lies its virtue: strategy without solvency is fantasy. The forecast ensures survival long enough to pursue broader aims. It buys time and mental clarity. It rescues the solo business owner from the tyranny of uncertainty.

The lingering question is whether leaders will embrace its discipline. For many, pride resists: isn't a business meant to operate on grander horizons? Yet history and lived experience whisper otherwise. Empires, like enterprises, often fell not from lack of ambition but from neglect of the near term—the missed supply convoy, the exhausted treasury, the bill unpaid. The two-week forecast asks: can you see two weeks ahead? If the answer is yes, the future beyond it becomes far easier to shape.

Buffers, Buckets, and Owner Pay

A strange truth runs through the lives of many small business owners: they can run successful enterprises, serve loyal clients, even report tidy profits—and yet feel personally poorer and more precarious than their salaried peers. The paradox is not always a matter of income, but of structure. Without deliberate systems for separating obligations, protecting pay, and smoothing volatility, profit becomes a mirage. The accounts show health; the owner feels constant strain.

The simplest remedy is also the most powerful: create buffers and buckets. It is a method as old as the concept of stewardship itself, practised by households long before the rise of double-entry bookkeeping, and revived by modern behavioural finance in the language of envelopes, jars, and pots. At its core, the approach replaces the fog of one big balance with the clarity of several small, purposeful balances. Instead of a single pile of cash that promises everything and guarantees nothing, funds are divided into three homes: taxes, owner pay, and operations. One extra layer—a buffer—sits on top as insurance against the unpredictable.

Why does this work so well? Because money, left in a general pool, is psychologically liquid. It tempts overcommitment. The rent feels affordable until the tax bill lands. A new software subscription looks harmless until payroll collides with a slow-paying client. By contrast, money placed into a bucket is anchored. £1,000 marked "tax" is no longer discretionary; it is already spoken for. £2,500 tagged "owner pay" ceases to be a guilty withdrawal and becomes a rightful income. The bucket system does not increase cash; it increases confidence.

Case studies abound. A freelance videographer who adopted a three-bucket model described the change as "earning a salary for the first time in years." Previously, every client payment sat in one account. She would splurge in the flush weeks, then scramble during the lean ones. By automating a split—40 per cent to taxes, 30 per cent to personal pay, 30 per cent to operating expenses—she created an invisible discipline. Within three months, the volatility of her cash experience halved, even though total revenue had not shifted at all.

The buffer adds the final layer of calm. While the buckets enforce allocation, the buffer absorbs shocks. A target—say one month of fixed outgoings—acts as a financial firewall. It is not there to fund growth, but to prevent collapse. In practice, it buys time: the ability to wait for an invoice rather than beg, to weather a lull without panic. Owners who maintain a buffer describe the shift as almost existential: the constant hum of anxiety quiets because the business can breathe.

Critics sometimes dismiss these techniques as simplistic. Shouldn't a serious business rely on sophisticated forecasts, credit facilities, or nuanced treasury practices? The answer lies in scale. A solo professional or micro-enterprise does not need Wall Street tools; they need repeatable rituals that work in minutes. Automation strengthens the habit. Many modern banks allow rules: every deposit can be split on arrival, with predetermined percentages flowing into separate buckets. The discipline is no longer dependent on willpower. The buckets fill, invisibly, while the owner focuses on work.

The deeper point is philosophical. Guarding cash is not only about avoiding overdraft fees; it is about shaping identity. When an owner pays themselves predictably, they begin to see their labour as worthy of consistent reward. When taxes are set aside early, civic duty becomes less fraught. When operations are funded consciously, investments are evaluated against actual capacity, not fantasy. Each bucket reinforces a mode of thinking: responsibility, dignity, prudence.

The brilliance of the system also lies in how quickly stability appears. Unlike long-term strategies that take quarters to bear fruit, buckets and buffers transform the emotional climate of a business in weeks. The act of automation signals to the mind that chaos has been replaced with order. Even if the sums are modest, the framework scales. A £200 split is handled just as easily as £20,000. The owner experiences a through-line of control that transcends income volatility.

Yet there is an open question, one that haunts even the most disciplined systems: what happens when ambition outruns structure? A growing business will one day find its buckets inadequate, its buffer under pressure, its allocations outdated. This is the healthy tension the method creates—it exposes growth for what it really is, not just an opportunity but a strain on stability. Will the owner keep refining the buckets, or will they revert to chaos in the pursuit of expansion?

In the end, buffers and buckets do not just manage money; they manage attention. They reduce noise, protect decisions, and restore the owner's sense of calm. But they also pose a challenge: once you have stability, how will you use it? Will it fuel bold experiments, or will it tempt complacency? The answer lies not in the system itself, but in the discipline of the person who keeps filling it, week after week, trusting that clarity is the best foundation for confidence.

Bridging the Gap Ethically

There is a quiet shame that shadows many business owners, especially in the fragile early years. They deliver value, their clients are satisfied, yet behind the scenes cash has run thin. Rent looms, staff need paying, and the owner wonders if one more awkward email—"Could you possibly pay early?"—will strain a relationship already built on trust. This scenario is more common than many admit. But it need not be endured in silence, nor handled through desperate improvisation. There is a way to bridge the gap between cash in and cash out without eroding dignity or goodwill.

The paradox lies here: clients are often willing to accommodate fair structures, but providers hesitate to ask. They fear seeming unprofessional, or worse, desperate. Yet the very opposite is true. Clear, principled policies around deposits, milestone billing, and scope adjustments communicate strength. They tell clients, *this business values order, fairness, and continuity*. When framed ethically, cash policies protect not only the owner but also the client, who benefits from a partner resilient enough to deliver without distraction or collapse.

Take the example of a design consultancy that shifted from billing on project completion to a three-stage milestone system: 30 per cent upfront, 40 per cent at delivery of draft, 30 per cent at final handover. Cash stress halved almost overnight. The policy was introduced not as a plea but as a professional standard—framed around mutual accountability and continuity of service. Clients accepted it readily because it felt less like a cash grab and more like a guarantee of steady focus. Ethical framing is everything.

Deposits, too, change the psychological contract. A deposit is not just a financial buffer; it signals commitment on both sides. Without it, projects drift, cancellations rise, and the provider shoulders all early risk. With it, energy aligns. The client has skin in the game, and the provider secures resources with confidence. For freelancers and micro-businesses, even modest deposits—20 or 30 per cent—can mean the difference between surviving a slow month and spiralling into crisis.

Then there is the matter of scope trims. In lean times, many owners feel pressured to discount prices to accelerate cash inflow. But a disciplined alternative exists: keep prices intact, trim scope instead. Offering a "lite" version of the service—one fewer revision cycle, a shorter workshop, a smaller deliverable—preserves value perception while easing the client's budget and improving the provider's cash cycle. Both sides keep dignity intact: the client still invests, and the provider avoids undermining their own worth.

Ethics run deeper than tactics. They are expressed in how these practices are communicated. An email begging for early payment is fraught with undertones of fragility; a policy shared in advance is simply professional hygiene. Scripts matter. Phrasing like, "To ensure projects run smoothly and resources are reserved for you, we schedule deposits at the outset," is worlds apart from, "We're tight on cash this month—could you help by paying early?" One respects boundaries; the other collapses them.

Some argue that flexibility is more "human," that rigid policies can alienate clients. There is truth in this, but boundaries are what make relationships durable. Clients who value quality respect structure. The alternative—ad-hoc pleading, ever-shifting terms—erodes trust. Cash policies, when consistently applied, reduce awkwardness by removing it from the realm of personal favour. They become part of the rules of engagement, not the exception.

At a philosophical level, bridging the cash gap ethically affirms a principle often neglected in business discourse: resilience is relational. A business that collapses under the weight of its own disorder harms not only its owner but its clients, employees, and partners. By setting policies that protect continuity, the owner is not privileging self-interest at others' expense; they are sustaining the ecosystem. Ethics and pragmatism converge.

Scripts and systems cannot eliminate the natural volatility of business, but they can transform how that volatility is absorbed. A predictable rhythm of deposits cushions the troughs. Milestone billing ensures cash follows effort, not just completion. Scope trims align ambition with affordability. Together, these tools allow the owner to move from a position of constant reaction to one of principled response.

Still, a tension lingers. What happens when an owner enforces ethical policies, yet faces clients accustomed to looser arrangements? Will they walk away? Perhaps. But here lies the real test: is stability worth more than volume? For many, the answer must be yes. Cash health without dignity corrodes slowly; dignity without cash collapses quickly. The art lies in holding both.

Ultimately, bridging the gap ethically is not a matter of clever tactics but of identity. Does the business see itself as a dignified partner, entitled to clear terms and mutual respect, or as a supplicant dependent on the goodwill of others? Each invoice and policy is a chance to answer. The question remains, and it is one every owner must wrestle with: when the next gap appears—as it inevitably will—will you reach for ad-hoc favours, or will you trust in the principles you've set? The resilience of your enterprise may hang on that choice.

Chapter 6
Invoicing, Receipts, and the Frictionless File

Every small business owner has felt it—the uneasy silence after a project is finished but before the invoice is sent. Days slip by, then weeks, not because the client is unwilling to pay but because the act of invoicing has been delayed. It is not negligence, nor a lack of professionalism; it is a friction point in the system. Each delay quietly erodes cash flow, each forgotten receipt undermines records, and each unreconciled statement introduces doubt into the numbers. What begins as administrative hesitation accumulates into a structural weakness.

Consider the paradox: the work itself may be creative, efficient, even masterful, yet payment lags because the administrative infrastructure is fragile. The paradox cuts both ways. A business with strong invoicing, receipt capture, and reconciliation habits can appear smoother, more trustworthy, more established—sometimes more so than rivals whose core work is actually stronger. In other words, order in the paperwork often translates directly into perceived authority.

History provides a curious echo. Merchants of Renaissance Florence were not only pioneers of banking and trade but also of record-keeping discipline. The famed Medici ledgers were not incidental: they were the infrastructure that enabled ambition. Without systematic invoices, receipts, and reconciliations, their empire would have been unsustainable. Five centuries on, the principle remains unchanged. A business that cannot retrieve a receipt instantly, or hesitates over reconciling accounts, risks not only inefficiency but credibility.

The challenge for the modern one-person business is not ignorance of these tools but the cognitive and emotional weight they carry. Invoices feel like self-promotion, receipts like clutter, reconciliation like risk of exposure. Left unaddressed, these feelings turn what should be five-minute routines into week-long postponements. The key insight is that these frictions are not signs of character flaws—they are signals that the process itself needs redesign. Rhythm, automation, and a clear single source of truth transform bookkeeping from avoidance to calm habit.

This chapter builds around four pillars. First, the rhythm of invoicing: anchoring billing not to mood or memory but to milestones and calendar cues. Second, receipts as captured at source, dissolving the scavenger hunt that drains hours during tax season. Third, reconciliation as a simple three-step ritual, stripped of fear and error. And fourth, the single source of truth: a file system so intuitive that retrieval becomes instantaneous, crises vanish, and confidence compounds.

The significance reaches beyond mechanics. Timely invoicing is not only about being paid sooner; it signals professionalism and steadiness to the client. Efficient receipt capture is not only about tax compliance; it affirms self-respect, the quiet order of a business run cleanly. Reconciliation without anxiety is not only about avoiding mistakes; it rewires the relationship with numbers into one of trust. A frictionless file is not merely tidy storage; it is an intellectual architecture that sustains clarity in the face of chaos.

These practices address an undercurrent of modern business life: the hidden emotional toll of disorganisation. Anxiety does not always spring from market risk or client demands. Often, it is born of unanswered questions—*Did I send that invoice? Will I be able to find that receipt? Can I trust these numbers?* Each unresolved item eats at attention and undermines momentum. Systems dissolve these doubts not by demanding perfection but by reducing the number of decisions that rely on memory and willpower.

To grasp the payoff, picture two businesses with identical revenues and costs. One owner invoices at project close, captures receipts ad hoc, and dreads reconciliation. The other invoices on set dates, has receipts auto-forwarded and filed, reconciles weekly, and can retrieve any document in seconds. Their profit lines are identical on paper, yet in practice one is constantly distracted by admin anxiety while the other enjoys the freedom to think strategically. The difference is invisible to outsiders but profound for the owner's mental state and long-term capacity.

What follows is not a catalogue of software features or accounting theory but a reframing of administration itself—as infrastructure, not afterthought. If done right, invoicing and filing do not feel like chores; they feel like investments in clarity. If neglected, they quietly tax the business with stress, missed opportunities, and compromised credibility. The reward for mastery is not just efficiency but a form of ease, the calm confidence that the numbers will hold when tested.

The real question lingers: can you design your financial systems so that they are lighter to run than to avoid? This chapter argues yes. And once friction disappears, momentum takes its place. The business that once stumbled over paperwork begins to glide. What begins as a discipline of files and invoices becomes a foundation for ambition, stability, and trust.

Designing an Invoicing Rhythm

Every freelancer or small business owner has experienced it: the quiet unease that comes when work has been delivered but no invoice has been sent. The paradox is striking. The hardest part—creating, designing, building, serving—has been done. Yet the final step, requesting payment, stalls. Days turn into weeks, not because the client refuses to pay, but because the rhythm of invoicing has collapsed into hesitation. It is tempting to frame this as a personal flaw, as procrastination or even embarrassment. But in truth, it is not a flaw of character. It is a flaw of process.

Consider the analogy with musicians. A jazz quartet may rehearse for hours, but unless they anchor their rhythm, the performance collapses into noise. Timing is not simply a technical detail; it is the structure that allows expression to flourish. Invoicing operates the same way. Without rhythm, cash flow drifts. With rhythm, it becomes music—predictable, reliable, and sustaining.

Modern data confirms this. Research on small business failures consistently cites cash flow disruption as the most common cause, even above lack of demand or poor strategy. But behind "cash flow disruption" often lies a mundane fact: invoices are sent late, sporadically, or without anchors. In other words, the problem is not financial illiteracy but behavioural design. The owner has not created a system where invoicing is as natural and inevitable as brushing one's teeth.

The most powerful shift comes when invoicing is anchored not to willpower or mood, but to external cues: project milestones and calendar routines. A milestone-based rhythm might mean an invoice at project start, one at halfway, and one on delivery. A calendar-based rhythm might mean invoices are always sent on Fridays before 3 p.m. or the last working day of the month. The anchor matters less than the consistency. By moving the decision outside memory and into structure, the burden of choice disappears.

Templates amplify this rhythm. Many avoid invoicing because each bill feels like reinventing the wheel: formatting, wording, attaching terms. Templates dissolve that load. With a pre-set design—branded, clear, standardised—the act of invoicing shrinks to the simple task of filling in a date, an amount, and a name. Friction vanishes. The speed with which invoices go out is often the difference between being paid in days versus weeks. And speed compounds: earlier invoicing means earlier reminders, which means earlier payments.

The rhythm also has a psychological benefit. Sending invoices late fosters subconscious guilt, as though one is chasing the client or exposing disorganisation. Sending them promptly reframes the act as professional courtesy: the signal that the work is complete, that boundaries are clear, and that trust runs both ways. Clients read timing. An invoice sent promptly suggests competence and reliability. A delayed invoice, even when harmless, suggests disarray.

Yet the resistance to invoicing is not irrational. Many owners quietly confess to discomfort: it feels like asking for money, and asking for money feels awkward. But here lies a crucial reframe: invoicing is not asking, it is closing a loop. The client has already agreed to pay; the invoice is merely the instrument that allows them to do so. By embedding invoices into rhythm—milestones and calendars—one removes the psychological sting. It becomes automatic, even invisible, just as musicians count beats without thinking.

The long-term impact of rhythm is profound. Late invoices ripple into cash shortages, overdraft risk, and reactive borrowing. A simple routine—invoice on completion, or invoice on the 25th of every month—prevents crises before they begin. More subtly, it restores attention. The owner who is not worrying about overdue invoices is free to focus on sales, craft, or strategy. The rhythm is not just financial hygiene; it is cognitive liberation.

One-person businesses often imagine systems are for corporations, but rhythm is the simplest system of all. A calendar reminder, a recurring task in a to-do app, a dedicated "invoicing hour" each week—these small scaffolds build discipline without effort. Once rhythm is in place, invoicing ceases to be a task you dread and becomes a habit you trust.

What emerges is not merely efficiency but dignity. The professional who invoices consistently communicates self-respect and stability. Clients, whether consciously or not, respond to that steadiness. And the owner, freed from the guilt of delay, begins to associate invoicing not with avoidance but with progress—the satisfying signal that value has been delivered and acknowledged.

The unanswered question lingers: if invoicing rhythm is such a simple lever, why do so many businesses ignore it? The answer lies in inertia. Most accept the status quo until crisis forces change. But the wiser path is pre-emptive: to design rhythm now, before cash is strained, before credibility is questioned. The rhythm of invoicing is not a trivial detail. It is one of the most powerful, least appreciated drivers of financial health and professional authority. The only question is whether you will allow rhythm to emerge by design—or by the hard lessons of delay.

Receipts: Capture at Source

There are few moments in business more demoralising than the midnight search for a missing receipt. You know it exists: the train ticket bought for a client meeting, the software subscription that renewed last month, the meal with a prospective partner. Yet when the time comes—an audit, a tax return, a loan application—it is nowhere to be found. Hours are wasted rifling through inboxes, scrolling endlessly through PDF downloads, or opening crumpled envelopes at the bottom of a desk drawer. The frustration is not only logistical but existential. How can such small slips of paper hold such disproportionate power over one's time, confidence, and composure?

The paradox is sharp. Modern businesses often run on cutting-edge tools: cloud platforms, automation, predictive analytics. Yet at their core, many still fall prey to a medieval weakness: receipts that scatter into the ether. A missing invoice can derail a tax filing, inflate an accountant's bill, or even lead to penalties. And the injustice of it is clear—the money has already been spent. The transaction is real. But without proof, the business must pay again in time, energy, or fines.

The answer is deceptively simple: capture at source. The moment a receipt arrives—whether through email, a payment terminal, or a paper slip—it must enter a single, reliable system. No piles, no shoeboxes, no "I'll do it later." Every delay compounds friction. Every act of capture compounds order.

The most powerful techniques lean on automation rather than memory. Auto-forwarding email receipts into a dedicated "receipts@" inbox removes the burden of remembering. Camera-to-cloud apps allow paper receipts to be photographed and instantly tagged. The principle is universal: capture once, name once, never hunt again. With such a system, a future audit is reduced to a search query, not a nightmare.

Consider the accountant's perspective. A client hands over a year's worth of records: some scanned, some missing, others buried in email threads. The accountant must charge for hours of detective work. Contrast this with a client who delivers a neatly named, cloud-based folder where every transaction is present, dated, and searchable. The accountant's bill shrinks, the return is filed faster, and the client appears professional and prepared. The system pays for itself, often many times over.

There is also a profound psychological effect. When receipts are scattered, they lurk in the background, nagging at attention. Each purchase whispers: *Don't forget me.* When receipts are captured at source, that whisper disappears. Cognitive load lightens. Anxiety recedes. The business owner can trust that past transactions are securely archived and focus instead on the future.

Critics sometimes dismiss such systems as overkill for a small business. Why obsess over receipts when the sums are modest? Yet this misses the larger truth. The discipline of capturing at source is less about the size of the transaction than the quality of attention. The process affirms a principle: *every piece of financial evidence matters, and future-you deserves clarity, not chaos.* What looks like efficiency is, at heart, respect for one's own time.

Technology amplifies the principle. Cloud storage services now allow instant tagging and naming conventions—vendor, date, category—so that retrieval becomes trivial. The search function replaces the shoebox. A five-second habit at the point of purchase can save five hours a year. And for businesses facing audits, the difference is existential: from panic to calm, from scrambling to control.

There is a deeper philosophical point here. The human mind is ill-suited to act as a filing cabinet. Memory is precious and limited; wasting it on receipts is a tax on creativity and strategy. By outsourcing capture to systems—auto-forward rules, camera apps, structured folders—the entrepreneur honours memory's scarcity and reserves it for work that actually generates value. The system becomes a silent partner, one that quietly absorbs disorder and returns peace of mind.

The rhythm is simple but transformative: capture, name, store. Done consistently, it builds a living archive that grows without effort. Tax preparation becomes painless. Financial reviews become reliable. Hours are reclaimed each month. And the true beneficiary is not the tax authority or the accountant but the owner themselves, who inherits the serenity of order.

The open question remains: if capturing at source is so effective, why do so many resist? The answer is habit. Chaos is familiar, and discipline feels like effort. Yet the irony is that order, once installed, is *less* effort than disorder. The realisation often comes too late, in the midst of an audit or a tax deadline. But for those willing to act pre-emptively, the payoff is immediate. The work of today saves the hours of tomorrow. The smallest slip of paper, handled correctly, becomes not a liability but a promise kept to your future self.

Reconciliation Without Tears

Few buttons inspire as much dread in small business accounting software as the one labelled *Reconcile*. To the uninitiated it sounds benign, even positive—who wouldn't want their books reconciled? Yet for many, that single click has come to symbolise the prospect of exposure: missing payments, unexplained duplicates, PayPal transfers that seem to evaporate, Stripe fees that gnaw invisibly at margins. It feels less like balancing the books and more like standing trial before them.

The irony is striking. Reconciliation is one of the simplest concepts in finance: compare what your records say with what actually happened in your bank or payment processor, and make sure they align. In principle, it should be as straightforward as matching items on a shopping list against what's in your basket. But in practice—particularly in the world of one-person businesses where personal accounts, multiple platforms, and foreign currency charges weave together—the list rarely matches. The gap between theory and lived experience fuels avoidance. The reconcile button gathers dust, and with it grows an invisible anxiety.

What transforms this moment of dread into one of calm is not more complexity but less. Reconciliation only becomes painful when it is approached haphazardly. When given a repeatable system, it reveals itself as one of the most powerful trust-building habits in business. A three-step checklist, executed weekly, strips the task of drama and turns reconciliation into a quiet confirmation: yes, your numbers are real.

The first step is direct matching: take each transaction recorded in your books and line it against the bank or processor feed. Money out, money in, like for like. The vast majority of items—rent payments, subscriptions, invoices—will align instantly. The second step is categorising anomalies. Here, the business owner resists the temptation to "fix as you go" and instead shunts edge cases into their own dedicated lane: Stripe fees that offset an invoice, PayPal transfers between currencies, or pending card holds. By naming these exceptions and giving them their own category, one removes their sting. They are no longer lurking mysteries but recognised residents of a separate bucket.

The third step is clearance. Every week, decide the fate of the edge cases. Some resolve automatically when the delayed charge posts; others require a one-line adjustment or a note for the accountant. Crucially, nothing is left unacknowledged. The inbox of exceptions is cleared just as the financial inbox is cleared. The power of this system lies less in its technicality than its ritual. Once mastered, reconciliation becomes less a test and more a small weekly ceremony that affirms order.

Real-world case studies underline the point. One consultant, who had avoided reconciliation for six months, discovered through this method that half of her apparent revenue shortfall was simply Stripe fees unrecorded against invoices. Another small e-commerce owner, who had once treated PayPal as a swamp of uncertainty, created a dedicated "PayPal Transit" account in her books. Every transfer in or out moved through this lane, creating visibility. Suddenly the reconcile button no longer threatened to reveal chaos; it confirmed the story already told.

Philosophically, reconciliation speaks to something deeper than bookkeeping. It addresses our discomfort with reality checks. Many avoid looking too closely at their finances for fear of what they might find. Yet the act of matching transactions with bank feeds is, in its essence, an act of truth-telling. It insists that business numbers are not abstractions but reflections of lived flows of money. The relief that follows is not merely financial but existential: the numbers are no longer enemies but mirrors.

Critics sometimes argue that reconciliation is unnecessary if one trusts their accounting software's automated feeds. But blind trust in automation is itself a risk. Banks occasionally misclassify, APIs fail, duplicates creep in. Without reconciliation, errors accumulate silently. With it, even the errors gain context—they are surfaced, quarantined, resolved. Far from being redundant, reconciliation is the layer of verification that ensures automation remains trustworthy.

The long-term effect is confidence. When books are reconciled, decisions can be made without the nagging doubt that the foundation may be flawed. Taxes can be estimated accurately. Cash flow forecasts gain solidity. An investor or lender who asks for statements sees clean alignment rather than hesitant explanations. The reconcile button no longer triggers anxiety but closure.

The open challenge is this: why, knowing its value, do so many still avoid it? Perhaps because reconciliation exposes the places where attention has been lacking. But this is precisely why it must become habitual. Each small reconciliation is a rehearsal for facing facts quickly, rather than allowing uncertainty to metastasise. Over time, what was once feared becomes freeing.

The choice remains in front of every business owner: will the reconcile button continue to symbolise avoidance, or can it be reimagined as a weekly gesture of clarity? The system is simple, the discipline finite. What it demands is not technical expertise but the courage to look, regularly, at the truth of one's numbers—and to press that button without fear.

The Single Source of Truth

A frantic search for a missing invoice is rarely about the paper itself. It is about control—or the sudden absence of it. One-person business owners know the feeling too well: rifling through email threads, scrolling cloud folders at midnight, convinced that a tax inspector, auditor, or client will ask tomorrow for the one document that refuses to appear. In that moment, the weakness of a scattered system is exposed. The business may be profitable, its services valued, but the inability to retrieve a single file on demand undermines trust, both internal and external.

The paradox is simple: the smallest businesses often carry the greatest complexity in record-keeping. A freelancer may juggle PayPal statements, Stripe payouts, supplier receipts, and client contracts, each trapped in its own silo. What is lost is not just time but composure. Order exists in fragments, but not as a whole. And when order is fragmented, stress compounds. The real cost is not the 30 minutes wasted hunting for a receipt but the invisible drag on confidence, the erosion of decisiveness, the lingering sense that the ground is less solid than it should be.

What restores that confidence is the creation of a *single source of truth.* One system—simple, consistent, and universally applied—that houses every financial document: quotes, invoices, statements, contracts, receipts. When all materials live in one place, retrieval becomes instant. Search is trivial. More importantly, trust in the system grows with every successful retrieval. This is not about digital housekeeping. It is about reclaiming mental bandwidth and ensuring that your financial world operates with the elegance of a well-run archive rather than the chaos of a scavenger hunt.

In practice, the shift is less technical than behavioural. Cloud storage makes it possible; discipline makes it reliable. A single folder structure, mirrored across devices, removes ambiguity. Client quotes go in one folder, invoices in another, receipts in a third. Subfolders track years or projects. Standardised naming conventions transform files from amorphous attachments into instantly recognisable entries: "2025-03 ClientName Invoice.pdf" leaves no room for confusion. Templates accelerate the process further. The result is not a set of folders but a system that runs itself.

Case studies illustrate the stakes. One designer, after adopting a disciplined foldering system, cut his end-of-year tax preparation from three stressful days to a calm two hours. Another consultant, previously reliant on email search, discovered that a single lost invoice had cost her an entire month's cash inflow because she had delayed sending reminders without evidence to hand. With a unified system, the same reminder became a two-click exercise. What changed was not only efficiency but assertiveness: she could approach clients with confidence because the proof was always present.

Sceptics might argue that search tools are powerful enough to locate documents across inboxes and cloud drives. But the distinction lies in reliability. Relying on search means trusting algorithms to find what you already suspect exists. A single source of truth eliminates doubt altogether; it ensures that everything exists in one location, by design. Search becomes a convenience rather than a crutch. More importantly, during moments of pressure—an audit, a legal dispute, a time-sensitive client demand—certainty matters more than convenience.

Philosophically, this move speaks to a deeper instinct: the desire to impose order on chaos. Humans create libraries, not random piles of books. Archives, not boxes of loose papers. A single source of truth reflects the same logic. It is not merely about neatness but about narrative coherence. A well-structured folder system tells the story of a business without gaps. Each document is a sentence; together they form a legible whole. The clarity of that archive influences how one perceives the business itself: structured, transparent, dependable.

The cumulative effect is striking. Every time a document is captured, named, and stored correctly, future crises are pre-empted. The system compounds in value because every retrieval reinforces the habit. Instead of anxiety about the next audit or tax season, there is calm assurance that everything is already in place. The order extends beyond the files: it creates a subtle but powerful sense of professional maturity. A one-person business with disciplined records does not feel like a fragile endeavour; it feels like an organisation of substance.

And yet, the open question remains: why do so many resist creating this single source of truth, despite its obvious benefits? Perhaps because disorder has a deceptive immediacy: one can always "search later," "sort later," "find it when it matters." But later is precisely when the cost is highest. The choice, then, is not between filing and saving time—it is between filing now and panicking later.

A single source of truth is not a luxury; it is the infrastructure of trust. In the quiet order of a foldering system lies resilience. The invoices, receipts, and statements stop being scattered fragments and become a coherent whole. But the question still hangs for every business owner: will the next document you need appear instantly, or will it trigger another midnight search? The answer depends entirely on whether you have built the system—or whether you are still relying on luck.

Chapter 7
Pricing with Evidence

The quiet terror of naming a price has haunted traders, artisans, and professionals for centuries. A potter in an open-air market, hands still dusty from the wheel, might hesitate before quoting a sum to a curious stranger. A consultant today, asked for a proposal, may feel the same tightness in the throat before typing a number into an email. Across centuries and professions, the discomfort is less about arithmetic and more about uncertainty: is this figure justified, or merely guessed?

Pricing is often treated as an act of theatre—part performance, part gamble—rather than the disciplined process it ought to be. Many one-person businesses cling to round numbers plucked from air or copied from competitors, mistaking habit for strategy. Yet beneath every sale lies a set of hard facts: how much time a service consumes, how much cash it truly leaves behind after costs, and how fragile the margin becomes when chipped by discounts, deposits, or scope creep. Evidence is there, hiding in plain sight, but too rarely invited into the conversation.

The paradox is striking. Business owners who can explain their craft in precise detail often stumble when asked to articulate its value in financial terms. A designer may know every pixel of a logo, a coach every stage of transformation for their client, yet when pressed on price, instinct replaces data. The result is fragile pricing: vulnerable to negotiation, riddled with doubt, and incapable of scaling with confidence. Evidence—rigorous, practical, and human-centred—is what transforms this fragility into strength.

Consider the discipline of breaking a service into sellable units. A photography package is not an abstract "day rate" but a sum of hours, edits, equipment use, and travel. By surfacing contribution per unit, patterns emerge: which offerings sustain, which drain, which are busy but broke. In this light, pricing ceases to be a vague expression of worth and becomes a lever of design. The question shifts from "What can I get away with charging?" to "What packages deserve survival, growth, or retirement?" Numbers sharpen vision.

The same clarity extends to policies around discounts and deposits. A seemingly generous 10 per cent discount can erase more than half the profit if margins are thin. Deposits, meanwhile, are not about distrust but about stability: they anchor commitment for both sides, turning promises into predictable cash flow. Evidence reframes what feels awkward into what is necessary. Preventative fences against scope creep are not a defence against clients, but a defence of sustainability itself. With data, calm replaces conflict.

Experimentation, too, becomes less daunting when stripped of guesswork. A/B testing is not the preserve of Silicon Valley giants but a practical tool for the smallest service provider. Trialling two versions of a proposal, experimenting with anchor pricing, or offering a premium frame alongside a baseline option can reveal what intuition never could. Evidence replaces mythology. Over time, these micro-experiments compound into a body of knowledge uniquely tailored to one's business.

But even with numbers and tests, the act of *saying the number out loud* remains its own challenge. Here, confidence is not innate—it is rehearsed. Scripts reduce anxiety, silence after naming a price becomes a tool rather than a fear, and the spoken figure aligns at last with the value delivered. This is where evidence meets psychology: once a price is backed by proof, the weight of delivery feels lighter.

This chapter is not about pricing theory in the abstract. It is about dismantling the fog that surrounds what should be one of the clearest levers in a business. Each section translates evidence into action: grounding services in unit economics, defending margins with principled policies, experimenting with offers as a habit, and building confidence in the human act of naming a price.

The transformation is subtle but profound: pricing shifts from hunch to system, from guesswork to grounded judgement. Yet an open question remains: once evidence becomes the bedrock of pricing, will the discomfort of asking for money ever fully disappear—or is it the tension itself that keeps us honest, ensuring that numbers remain tethered to value?

Unit Economics for Humans

The strangest contradiction in modern freelancing and small business is this: one can be overwhelmed with work, every hour filled, yet find that profit remains elusive. Diaries brim with deadlines, inboxes overflow with projects, and still the bank balance refuses to reflect the labour invested. The paradox of being *busy but broke* is not a moral failing or a lack of effort—it is often the absence of a clear view of unit economics.

Imagine a craftsperson at a medieval fair, selling hand-carved spoons. Each one takes an hour to shape, polish, and present. If the selling price barely covers the wood and stall rent, then selling twice as many spoons only deepens the exhaustion. Yet from the crowd's vantage point, this vendor looks successful: the stall is bustling, the inventory moves quickly. Only the craftsman knows that beneath the surface, each transaction erodes rather than builds. The story has not changed. In today's knowledge economy, countless professionals still carve their metaphorical spoons without ever calculating whether the price of one unit sustains the life of the business.

Unit economics—the discipline of breaking down a service into measurable parts—is a tool to reveal these hidden truths. It asks: what does it cost, in both time and money, to deliver one unit of your service? What is the contribution left after direct costs are stripped away? Instead of drowning in aggregate numbers, it insists on zooming in to the granular. This lens is disarmingly simple yet profoundly clarifying. Once applied, it shows not only which services sustain the business, but which silently bleed it dry.

Consider a freelance copywriter who offers three packages: a blog post, a sales page, and a full website rewrite. By tracking time spent and direct costs—research, design subcontractors, revisions—she realises the blog posts deliver only £18 per effective hour, the sales pages £60, and the website rewrites £95. Without this clarity, she might continue producing blog posts endlessly, drawn by their regularity, while unknowingly sacrificing the opportunity to pursue higher-value work. With unit economics revealed, she can see plainly: some offerings are busywork disguised as revenue, others are profit engines.

The method is not restricted to freelancers. Small consultancies, micro-agencies, and even solo coaches benefit. A consultant billing clients for "strategy days" may discover that preparation, travel, and post-session support dilute what seemed a lucrative fee into something closer to subsistence. Conversely, a shorter, tightly defined advisory call may yield higher effective returns. What matters is not what the invoice says, but what remains after the hidden layers of delivery have been stripped back.

There is also a psychological dimension. Many business owners feel loyalty to long-standing services, even when those services are unsustainable. Retiring an offering can feel like betrayal—towards one's craft, or towards clients who have come to expect it. Yet when confronted with cold numbers, attachment yields to pragmatism. Here lies a philosophical lesson: true stewardship of a business means not only nurturing what you love, but pruning what drains vitality. Growth is not merely expansion but selection.

Critics sometimes argue that quantifying every aspect of work risks reducing creativity to arithmetic. Does breaking a service into units not strip it of its artistry? The counterpoint is simple: the act of measurement is not the end, but the means. By grounding pricing in reality, you free yourself from the anxiety of guesswork and preserve the space to be creative. Knowing that a service is profitable allows you to deliver it with confidence, rather than the quiet resentment that comes from undervaluation.

Tools for this practice can be modest: a spreadsheet logging hours against revenue, a habit of recording the true costs of subcontractors, software fees, or transaction charges. Over weeks, the data reveals patterns. Contribution per unit becomes visible. From there, three pathways emerge—raise, retire, or redesign. Raising means charging more for units that deliver value but are currently underpriced. Retiring means letting go of those that never justify their existence. Redesigning means reshaping delivery so the unit sustains both the client's needs and the provider's livelihood.

The beauty of unit economics is its fairness. It does not moralise about worth; it describes reality. It shows where labour translates into profit and where it does not. It respects memory as a scarce resource—rather than relying on intuition or recall, it builds a living record that accumulates truth. It asks us to acknowledge not just the sweat of effort, but the weight of outcomes.

And yet, one question lingers. Once the numbers reveal the uncomfortable fact that a beloved service is unprofitable, will the courage follow to act on it? Evidence grounds pricing, but evidence alone does not compel decision. It is in that fragile moment—between recognition and response—that a business's trajectory is defined. Will the owner cling to busyness, or embrace the discipline that finally transforms labour into livelihood?

Discounts, Deposits, and Scope Creep

The discount is one of the oldest gestures in commerce—part courtesy, part strategy, part surrender. A shopkeeper in an ancient market might shave a coin from the price to secure loyalty, or to close a sale before the buyer walked away. In that context, the loss felt tolerable: margins were wide, the transaction was immediate, the relationship face-to-face. But for today's freelancer or small firm, the hidden cost of even a modest discount is rarely so visible. A ten per cent cut does not simply trim ten per cent from earnings; it can obliterate the margin entirely. What feels like generosity in the moment can, when scaled across multiple projects, undermine the very sustainability of the business.

Consider this paradox. A consultant who charges £1,000 for a day's work with a £700 cost base—time, travel, preparation—retains £300 of profit. A ten per cent discount reduces the fee to £900, but the cost base remains the same. Profit falls not by ten per cent but by a third, from £300 to £200. If discounts become habitual, the consultant must now work significantly more days simply to stand still. This is the arithmetic that is so often disguised by the optics of goodwill. The client is pleased, the invoice is accepted, but the erosion accumulates silently.

The better alternative is rarely to lower the number, but to reshape the value. Instead of conceding price, add clarity of scope, offer faster delivery, or create tiered options that let the client self-select their trade-off. A photographer, asked to reduce their rate, can present a smaller package—half-day instead of full-day coverage, fewer edited images, quicker turnaround. The client feels agency, not charity, and the professional preserves margin while retaining dignity. This subtle reframing moves the conversation from "price" to "value," from concession to collaboration.

Deposits function as the quiet counterweight to discounts. Where discounts erode confidence and cash flow, deposits stabilise them. To require part-payment upfront is not arrogance but prudence. It acknowledges that commitment is mutual: the provider sets aside time and resources, the client secures priority. Deposits also transform cash flow from precarious to predictable. A designer who insists on 30 per cent upfront finds that invoices no longer languish unpaid for weeks; cash is banked at the start, and the psychological burden of uncertainty diminishes. More than money, deposits create trust. They signal seriousness. They reduce flakiness. They replace the unspoken worry—*will I actually be paid?*—with the assurance that the work has already been anchored.

Scope creep is perhaps the most insidious of the three forces. Unlike discounts, which are visible on the invoice, scope creep arrives disguised as small requests. "Could we just add one more feature?" "Would you mind making a few extra revisions?" "Could this include an additional report for the board?" Each feels too minor to resist, but collectively they distort timelines, consume energy, and dilute profitability. Over months or years, scope creep becomes a culture—an expectation that professionals will always absorb more for the same fee. It corrodes not only margins but morale.

The solution is not to clamp down with hostility but to construct preventative fences. Clear proposals, explicit deliverables, and pre-defined revision limits create boundaries that clients respect. Some professionals employ change order forms—simple, neutral documents that translate "just one more thing" into a new, priced item. Others adopt a softer but equally effective script: "Happy to add this—shall we adjust the scope or budget to reflect it?" Such phrasing avoids confrontation yet signals that value has limits. Calm replaces conflict, not because boundaries are absent, but because they are agreed in advance.

At a deeper level, these practices touch on the philosophy of self-respect in business. To discount reflexively is to undervalue oneself. To avoid deposits is to accept risk without reciprocity. To allow unchecked scope creep is to silently consent to exploitation. Each decision, small in isolation, compounds into a culture—one either of erosion or of equilibrium. Professionals who enforce thoughtful policies are not rigid; they are sustainable. Their calmness in negotiation stems from systems, not from posturing.

There is, however, a tension that remains unresolved. Clients often expect flexibility, and markets reward responsiveness. The line between principled firmness and perceived inflexibility is thin. When does protecting margin and dignity become self-sabotage, pushing clients away? When does generosity cease to be strategy and become self-harm? The answers are not universal, and therein lies the challenge. Each professional must calibrate their own equilibrium—between service and sustainability, between generosity and self-respect. The arithmetic of discounts, deposits, and scope may be simple; the ethics of their application remain complex. And it is precisely within this tension that the art of business resides.

A/B Your Offers

Every entrepreneur knows the restless anxiety of setting a price. Raise it, and you risk losing the sale. Lower it, and you risk losing your margin. Most fall back on instinct, imitation, or inertia. Yet history shows that markets reward not the boldest guesser, but the quiet experimenter. In the 1950s, direct mail catalogues began running different offers to different households—one group received a £5 discount, another free shipping, another a premium add-on. The companies didn't guess which worked; they measured. The most successful offers scaled, the failures were discarded, and what seemed a matter of hunch became a matter of evidence. The principle, now called A/B testing, has long since escaped the world of mail-order catalogues and landed squarely in the toolkit of digital business.

The paradox is that while giants like Amazon or Booking.com run thousands of pricing experiments each year, the solo professional often runs none. A freelancer may agonise over whether to quote

£800 or £1,000 for a project, yet present only one version to the client and live with the uncertainty forever. The opportunity is not in predicting the perfect figure, but in building a habit of structured trials—small, ethical, reversible tests that reveal what the market really values. Evidence, not intuition, becomes the compass.

Consider three of the simplest levers: anchors, premium framing, and de-bundling. Anchoring exploits the well-documented psychological effect that the first number we see shapes our perception of value. A consultant who presents a £5,000 strategic package before a £2,500 operational package subtly reframes the latter as affordable, even though the figure itself has not changed. Premium framing uses a high-end option—sometimes aspirational, sometimes extravagant—to elevate the perceived worth of mid-tier offers. A photographer who adds a £10,000 "platinum" package may see sales rise in the £3,000 "gold" tier, even if no-one ever buys the platinum. De-bundling, conversely, reveals the value of components when separated. A coach offering a full programme at £2,400 can test offering modules at £800 each; some clients will prefer to buy step by step, others will see the full package as more economical. In each case, the professional does not rely on speculation but gathers data.

The effect of these micro-experiments is often disproportionate. In one study of SaaS pricing, companies that regularly tested their price structures grew revenue nearly twice as fast as those that set and forgot. For small service firms, even one successful trial—say, discovering that a deposit combined with a modest premium option lifts average sales by 15 per cent—can change the trajectory of their financial stability. And unlike massive corporate tests, these require no complex software. Two versions of a proposal, two tiers on a website, two scripts for a sales call—each conversation becomes a site of learning.

The deeper insight is not merely that evidence is better than guessing, but that experimentation itself is a discipline worth cultivating. To A/B your offers is to resist the illusion of permanence. Prices are not monuments; they are hypotheses. Every proposal is a test of perception, positioning, and value. Those who treat pricing as static risk becoming fossilised, while those who treat it as a living experiment stay in dialogue with their market.

There are, of course, tensions. Clients may notice differences, and questions of fairness arise. Is it ethical to quote two clients slightly differently to learn what the market bears? Some argue that transparency demands uniformity. Others counter that value is inherently contextual—that urgency, scope, and client capacity shape worth. Here, too, the professional must decide where to draw the line between research and opportunism.

What remains constant is the compounding effect of curiosity. A single A/B test provides a datapoint; a year of them provides a map. Over time, the professional becomes less anxious, because they are no longer relying on fragile intuition but on lived evidence. The client conversation shifts too. Instead of faltering after naming a price, the professional speaks with the quiet confidence of one who has tested, learned, and iterated.

Yet an unresolved question lingers: does the relentless search for the "optimal" offer risk reducing human relationships to experiments? Is there a point at which the quest for efficiency erodes the trust and warmth that make commerce more than transaction? The answer may not be final. But what is clear is this: professionals who experiment thoughtfully, with integrity, build not just higher sales, but sharper judgement. The habit of testing becomes not merely a tool of commerce, but a mindset of resilience. And perhaps that, more than any single price point, is what truly accelerates learning.

Saying the Number Out Loud

The room often falls silent at the very moment it matters most. A consultant, coach, or designer outlines their proposal with clarity, narrates the value they bring, and then arrives at the sentence that decides whether the conversation turns into business or evaporates into awkwardness. "The fee for this project is..." Their voice falters, the number sounds apologetic, and they rush to fill the silence with justifications, caveats, or nervous chatter. What might have been a confident declaration becomes an opening for doubt, negotiation, or retreat.

Why does articulating a number out loud feel so different from writing it down? The same professional who can produce a meticulously calculated spreadsheet suddenly feels like they are standing on trial. The reason is simple: numbers spoken aloud are not abstractions—they are performances of worth. They do not merely describe value; they embody it. To say a price is to announce, in public, what you believe your time, skill, and contribution are worth. That is why it carries such psychological weight.

The paradox is that the discomfort does not arise because the price is too high, but because the speaker has not rehearsed the act of saying it. Price anxiety is not cured by discounting or hedging; it is cured by practice. Musicians rehearse scales, athletes repeat drills, actors run their lines. Professionals, however, often expect confidence to arrive uninvited. They prepare their documents but not their voices. Yet confidence in pricing is not spontaneous—it is built through deliberate, structured rehearsal.

One powerful exercise is scripting. Not in the sense of robotic recitation, but in crafting a simple, declarative sentence and repeating it until it feels natural. "My fee for this scope is £3,000." Nothing more. The goal is not to embellish, soften, or disguise, but to normalise the act of naming the number. Many practitioners find it helpful to practise aloud in front of a mirror, into a voice recorder, or with a colleague acting as a mock client. Over time, what once triggered adrenaline becomes as routine as stating one's address.

The second exercise is silence. After naming the number, resist the urge to rush in. Silence may feel unbearable at first, but it is not a void—it is space for the client to process. Negotiation scholars have long noted that the first to fill the silence often loses ground. By holding steady, the professional communicates self-assurance. The client senses that the number has been considered, justified, and is not up for casual erosion. The stillness becomes its own form of persuasion.

Real-world examples illustrate the shift. A freelance developer once described how their income transformed when they stopped padding their price with nervous qualifiers like, "It's around £2,000, but I can adjust if that's too much." Clients sensed the hesitation and pushed for reductions. After practising a clean, silent delivery, the same £2,000 figure was accepted without question in most cases. The difference was not the number—it was the posture.

Yet there is a deeper philosophical thread here. To say the number out loud is to align external transaction with internal self-worth. Many professionals struggle with pricing not because of poor calculation, but because of doubt about their own value. The rehearsal, then, is not only about speaking clearly; it is about believing that the number reflects reality. When the spoken price resonates with the professional's sense of fairness and contribution, conversations simplify. Negotiations lose their combative edge. Both parties sense that the figure is neither inflated nor apologetic—it is simply true.

Of course, tension remains. What if the client genuinely cannot afford the number? What if the market pushes back repeatedly? These are not failures of delivery but signals to re-examine positioning, scope, or target audience. Confidence in saying the number should never be confused with stubbornness. The art is in combining grounded self-belief with empirical feedback. Spoken practice provides the steadiness; evidence and iteration provide the calibration.

What emerges is a discipline that blends psychology and economics. Numbers stop being abstract symbols on paper and become part of lived dialogue. Professionals who practise the ritual of saying them aloud build not just sales skill but resilience. They begin to see silence not as danger, but as respect. They learn that confidence is not an innate trait but a craft honed sentence by sentence.

And yet one unresolved question hovers in the background: if confidence is practised like any other skill, might underconfidence itself be a habit—one that has been rehearsed, silently, for years? If so, the choice to script, to rehearse, and to say the number out loud is more than a sales technique. It is the conscious unlearning of a habit of self-diminishment. What follows from that shift may reach far beyond pricing. It may shape how one speaks of their time, their boundaries, and their worth in every domain of life.

Chapter 8
The Monthly Close and the Owner's Debrief

At first glance, the close of a month feels arbitrary. Thirty or thirty-one days have passed; another calendar page turns. Yet for the owner of a business, the act of stopping to look back at that span of time is anything but arbitrary. It is a ritual of perspective. What looked chaotic in the fog of daily tasks reveals pattern when traced across a month. The numbers no longer whisper—they speak plainly. What once felt like a reactive scramble becomes an opportunity to steer with deliberation.

Consider the contrast with the weekly review. A week is intimate: a handful of invoices due, a short-term cash pinch, a looming decision about one client. Weekly reviews deliver granularity, but they rarely deliver altitude. The month, by contrast, is long enough for themes to emerge. It shows whether profits have held or slipped, whether the pipeline is swelling or draining, whether the tax man's shadow is looming larger than expected. The month allows the entrepreneur to zoom out without losing sight of the detail.

This perspective shift matters because it tempers reaction. In the heat of a single week, a lost sale or late payment feels catastrophic. Over a month, these small disruptions can be weighed against wins, efficiencies, or structural improvements. The close of a month disciplines the mind: not every ripple is a storm, not every setback demands panic. What matters is whether the ship is still pointed towards its intended horizon.

At the heart of this practice is a subtle but powerful principle: lessons compound only when recorded. Most owners, caught in the rush of execution, make the same mistakes twice. A forgotten tax estimate, a misjudged discount, an unchecked scope creep. But the monthly close invites a pause: write down one needle-moving lesson from the past thirty days. Capture not just numbers, but decisions, hurts, and surprises. This record is more than bookkeeping—it is an archive of lived strategy, a personal textbook written in the margins of real commerce. Over years, it becomes a kind of private MBA, dense with wisdom no classroom could compress.

The monthly close also addresses one of the entrepreneur's greatest anxieties: taxation. The fear of the unexpected bill has haunted small businesses across centuries. Yet the panic is rarely about the absolute size of the tax due—it is about the *not knowing*. By using monthly profit to compute conservative set-asides, and by automating those transfers into a separate bucket, the spectre of surprise fades. What was once a quarterly scramble becomes a calm, habitual act. Discipline, when designed properly, feels less like punishment and more like kindness to one's future self.

Patterns, lessons, and tax set-asides prepare the ground for a deeper discipline: quarterly themes. The month offers data; the quarter demands direction. By translating insights into a single theme for the next quarter—whether it is tightening client qualification, raising one price, or streamlining delivery—the owner resists the lure of scattered ambition. Focus becomes the multiplier. Drift gives way to coherence. And when one theme compounds across a year, the results often outpace what a dozen disconnected initiatives could have achieved.

The debrief culminates in a practice at once simple and profound: writing a letter to your future self. One page, addressed not to investors or regulators, but to you. It notes what worked, what hurt, and what choices were made. It captures mood as well as metrics, the emotional truth alongside the financial. Over time, these letters form a dialogue across months and years, a lineage of thought and decision. They become a mirror more reliable than memory, a compass steadier than instinct. For the owner navigating alone, they offer a kind of company—the company of one's wiser, accumulated self.

The monthly close is therefore more than an administrative ritual. It is a form of self-governance, a check against drift, a space where numbers and narrative meet. It tames anxiety by replacing the unknown with the known. It turns repetition into refinement. And it quietly transforms the role of the owner: from firefighter reacting to sparks, to strategist steering by stars.

But here lies the unspoken tension: if the month reveals both patterns and pain, will the owner listen—or will they bury the lesson, repeating it anew? The power of the monthly close is not in the numbers alone but in the willingness to hear what they are saying. The chapter ahead explores how to listen, how to record, and how to translate those lessons into the kind of wisdom that endures.

From Weekly Granularity to Monthly Perspective

In 1961, when President John F. Kennedy demanded that America put a man on the moon, NASA engineers realised that precision was not the sole determinant of success. A rocket could be perfectly aligned at launch yet veer wildly off course within minutes. The solution was not constant micro-corrections—it was regular recalibration at wider intervals, guided by broader data. Weekly adjustments gave way to trajectories charted over longer arcs. The mission could succeed only if its leaders learned to step back, not just peer closer.

The same truth holds for business owners who live in the trenches of day-to-day detail. Weekly reviews deliver intimacy—who paid, what slipped, where the fires are burning. They are essential, but they can also distort. A missed invoice feels catastrophic. A single large expense feels fatal. Zoomed in too tightly, every ripple looks like a tidal wave. Step back, however, and the month reveals the ocean's actual current. It is in this shift—from weekly granularity to monthly perspective—that clarity deepens and reaction gives way to strategy.

The act of closing a month offers three lenses: the profit and loss statement, the cash calendar, and the sales pipeline. Each tells a story too large for the confines of a week. The P&L, stretched across thirty days, begins to surface trends—whether margins are eroding or holding, whether operating costs are creeping upward, whether revenue growth is real or illusory. The cash calendar shows whether inflows and outflows are aligning with reality or drifting into dangerous mis-timings. And the pipeline, often overlooked in the heat of a single week, reveals whether the future is quietly drying up or quietly compounding.

This expanded horizon tempers emotion. A bad week might see cash levels dip alarmingly; a good week might flood accounts with invoices cleared. Both events can distort judgement if taken in isolation. The monthly perspective places them in context: that late-paying client's delay was painful, but offset by two new engagements; that sudden surge of sales is real, but the margin attached reveals it to be far less exciting than it first appeared. Perspective is not detachment—it is disciplined proportion.

A subtle but vital addition to the monthly review is the practice of recording a single needle-moving lesson. Weeks blur. Without a marker, insights vanish as quickly as they appear. By capturing one distilled lesson—"raising prices halved workload but held revenue", or "failing to chase invoices cost a week's buffer"—the owner creates a chain of hard-earned wisdom. These lessons compound, and in time they form a library of decisions, turning mistakes into assets and patterns into policy.

The difference between weekly and monthly reviews can be likened to navigating with a torch versus a lantern. The torch illuminates the immediate path; it prevents tripping over the next stone. The lantern reveals the terrain, the slope, the direction of travel. Both are essential, but without the lantern, the traveller risks circling endlessly in the dark.

There is, of course, tension in stepping back. The owner accustomed to granular detail may resist the abstraction of a P&L, distrust the broader strokes of a pipeline forecast, or feel exposed when numbers no longer bend under the weight of excuses. Yet it is precisely this discomfort that makes the monthly close indispensable. It exposes structural truths—the ones too slow-moving to appear in the week's swirl, yet too powerful to ignore.

The shift also changes the role of the owner. In the weekly mode, they are firefighter and clerk, chasing, correcting, and reacting. In the monthly mode, they become strategist and steward, noting not just what happened, but why, and how it might shift in the months to come. This is not to dismiss weekly granularity; it is to recognise that without the scaffolding of monthly perspective, granularity becomes noise without music.

But here lies the lingering question: when the month lays bare its patterns—profit slipping, pipeline thinning, cash gaps widening—will the owner have the courage to act, or will they retreat into the false safety of weekly busyness? Numbers tell, but they cannot compel. The monthly close offers not certainty, but choice. What the owner does with that choice is what ultimately determines whether the business drifts, or whether it steers.

Tax Estimates Without Panic

Few moments in the life of a small business owner strike more dread than the arrival of the brown envelope from the tax authority. It is rarely the numbers themselves that cause the fear—it is the *not knowing*. A bill expected is a bill absorbed. A bill imagined is a spectre that grows in the mind until it dwarfs reality. For many, tax time is not a question of affordability but of surprise, of being caught off guard by obligations that were visible all along yet never truly confronted.

There is a paradox here worth naming. Taxes are the single most predictable expense in business, yet they are the one that most consistently provokes panic. The rules are published, the rates are known, the deadlines fixed. And still, each quarter or year, owners find themselves scrambling, borrowing, or explaining to accountants why the money isn't there. The mystery is not in the mathematics but in the psychology: tax feels abstract until it is immediate. It is both invisible and inevitable.

The antidote is not heroic effort at year-end but quiet, disciplined ritual built into the rhythm of the business. At its heart is the practice of setting aside a portion of rolling profit into a dedicated bucket—untouchable, automated, and conservative by design. This simple move transforms the tax bill from an ambush into a scheduled meeting. Anxiety drops, not because the liability is smaller, but because it is already funded. The unknown vanishes, and discipline reveals itself not as punishment but as protection.

The mechanics are straightforward. First, calculate a conservative percentage of profit—slightly higher than your effective tax rate.

Better to overshoot modestly and find a surplus than to underestimate and face a shortfall. Each week or month, as profit is computed, siphon this set-aside into a separate account. The transfer should be automatic, removing the burden of willpower. Over time, this tax bucket grows into a financial shock absorber, a quiet reserve that insulates the business from the rhythm of statutory deadlines.

Consider the experience of an independent consultant who adopted this practice. For years, she dreaded the January scramble, often draining personal savings or postponing investments to cover the bill. When she began setting aside 30% of her rolling profit into a separate account, the panic evaporated. She stopped treating the tax bill as a sudden loss and began seeing it as an ordinary transfer from one pocket to another. By the end of the year, her perspective had shifted: taxes had become routine, not rupture.

This reframing is more than mechanical; it is philosophical. It is about reclassifying tax from a *threat* to a *known cost of doing business*. In the same way a pilot learns to expect turbulence, the owner who builds tax set-asides into their routine learns to expect the obligation without dread. The discipline here is not ascetic. It is kind. It removes the cognitive load of anticipation, allowing energy to be spent on growth rather than anxiety.

There is also a broader truth: business resilience is built not in grand gestures but in small automatisms. Automating tax transfers is one such automatisation. It aligns with the psychology of "paying yourself first" but turns it outward, honouring obligations before they loom. For the sole trader or small business owner, this ritual becomes an act of self-respect. It is a promise kept to the future self, sparing them the humiliation of pleading with banks or deferring bills to satisfy the taxman.

Of course, discipline has its tensions. The temptation to raid the tax bucket in lean months is real, and resisting it requires both structural barriers and internal resolve. Some owners open accounts with withdrawal restrictions or label them explicitly as "do not touch". Others make it a matter of pride, reframing the untouched bucket as evidence of professionalism. Whatever the tactic, the underlying principle is the same: separate the money so that you can separate the emotion.

The irony is that once tax panic is removed, owners often discover a secondary benefit: clarity. Freed from the mental fog of anxiety, they begin to see profit more cleanly, to plan investments with greater confidence, to negotiate with less desperation. The tax bucket becomes not just a financial tool but a psychological one. It grants the owner space to act from strength rather than fear.

And yet, one question lingers. If taxes can be tamed through set-asides and automatisms, what other anxieties in business are the product not of reality but of avoidance? What other predictable obligations—insurance, equipment replacement, even retirement savings—could be rendered painless by the same logic? Tax may be the first and most urgent example, but it may also be the doorway to a broader practice: transforming inevitabilities into rituals, and turning dread into discipline. The answer lies not in numbers, but in the owner's willingness to replace panic with pattern.

Quarterly Themes

There is a seduction in ambition. The blank canvas of a new quarter tempts business owners into sprawling lists of goals, each one justified, each one urgent. But in practice, breadth dilutes depth. Energy fragments, progress diffuses, and the quarter ends in exhaustion rather than achievement. The paradox is clear: by trying to improve everything at once, nothing moves decisively.

History offers its own reminder. When President Kennedy declared the goal of putting a man on the moon within a decade, it was not one among a hundred priorities—it became *the* national theme. Resources, research, and willpower converged. The focus was radical, and as a result, momentum compounded. In business, the same logic applies. A single theme, owned and pursued for ninety days, yields more real change than a dozen well-meaning projects competing for attention.

The practice of quarterly themes is disarmingly simple. At the close of each cycle, review the data, the lessons, the frictions. Instead of drafting an exhaustive agenda, extract one theme that cuts deepest. It might be "lift gross margin by 3%", or "automate invoicing", or "stabilise client acquisition channels". The power lies in stripping away noise until only one lever remains. Focus beats ambition, not by denying ambition, but by sequencing it.

Consider the solo designer who found herself pulled in five directions: expanding her services, launching a course, revising her pricing, chasing overdue invoices, and upgrading her portfolio. Each initiative had merit, but together they produced paralysis. When she imposed a quarterly theme—"price clarity"—her horizon narrowed. She revised her offers, tested a new anchor, and scripted her pricing conversations. By quarter's end, revenue per project had risen by 18%. The other projects waited, but her business moved forward in a way it never had before.

A quarterly theme acts like a compass in the fog. It does not eliminate uncertainty, but it keeps movement consistent. Each decision can be filtered through the lens of alignment: does this serve the theme, or distract from it? Even in the mess of daily operations, direction emerges. The theme anchors ambition in discipline.

Sceptics may argue that narrowing to one focus risks neglecting other vital functions. But in reality, business health depends less on constant tinkering than on concentrated breakthroughs. One quarter spent streamlining outflows, another refining marketing language, another stabilising cash flow—across a year, the compound effect is dramatic. Momentum builds not in bursts, but in layers, each theme laying foundation for the next.

There is also a philosophical undertone. Quarterly themes embody the discipline of acceptance: recognising that you cannot do everything now, but you can do something that matters deeply. This is the antidote to drift. Without themes, quarters blur into one another, effort expends itself without accumulation, and the owner feels busy but unchanged. With themes, direction becomes visible, momentum tangible.

The practice demands courage. To pick one theme is to say no to others, and that "no" feels costly. Yet it is precisely this narrowing that yields clarity. The quarterly theme is not a denial of possibility—it is a wager on what will matter most. And if chosen wisely, the bet pays not just in results but in relief. Stress falls when the owner knows what to focus on and, more importantly, what to ignore.

Still, a tension remains. How does one resist the pull of new urgencies mid-quarter? What happens when opportunities arise that don't fit the theme? The discipline is imperfect, always tested by temptation and circumstance. But perhaps that is its greatest virtue: it forces a reckoning with distraction, a continual return to intention.

In the end, quarterly themes are not simply a tool of planning but a practice of restraint. They remind the owner that progress is not made by scattering energy but by aligning it, quarter after quarter, until drift gives way to direction. The deeper question, then, is not whether to choose a theme, but whether we dare to hold to it long enough for momentum to reveal itself.

The Debrief Letter to Future You

There is a peculiar kind of wisdom that comes only with hindsight, yet most businesses squander it. Each cycle ends, and its lessons vanish with it—buried in forgotten emails, half-remembered conversations, and unmarked spreadsheets. What worked is left uncelebrated, what failed unexamined. The wheel spins again, and the owner returns to the same challenges, only slightly more fatigued, slightly more anxious. The paradox is sharp: the richest teacher in a business—the lived experience of its own operator—is consulted least.

Consider the naval captain of the eighteenth century, whose voyage reports not only guided future expeditions but also shaped naval doctrine for decades. Every storm endured, every supply shortage, every unexpected encounter was written with the intent that others might not repeat the same errors. Those logs were more than records; they were tools of survival. For the solo business owner today, the same principle applies. The debrief letter is a captain's log for commerce: a structured act of remembrance, designed not for compliance but for growth.

Writing to your future self may sound indulgent, but in practice it is radically pragmatic. At the end of a month or quarter, setting aside one page to record what worked, what hurt, and the decisions you made distils experience into knowledge. It creates institutional memory for a company of one. Without it, the lessons of today dissolve into the noise of tomorrow. With it, clarity compounds cycle by cycle.

There is also a psychological depth to the act. To write a debrief is to step outside the rush of immediacy and into the perspective of reflection. The process tempers reaction with understanding. A botched client negotiation, once written down with its context and outcome, becomes less of a personal failure and more of a case study. A marketing experiment that fell flat shifts from embarrassment to data point. The writing reframes experience, turning raw events into material for wisdom.

Imagine a freelancer who, every quarter, drafts a single page: *Revenue rose by 12% after focusing on retainer clients. Project X drained more hours than expected; next time, scope must be tighter. Began using templates for proposals—saved five hours this month. Overcommitted in July—don't repeat.* A year later, that archive is not a pile of notes but a private MBA. It reveals patterns invisible at the time: where profit consistently arises, where stress accumulates, which experiments paid off, and which traps recur. No seminar or textbook could replicate such specific, hard-won clarity.

There is a humility embedded in the debrief letter. It acknowledges that memory is porous, that the mind rationalises failures and embellishes victories. By writing now for your future self, you refuse the illusion that you will "just remember." The record becomes a dialogue across time: the past offering the future not platitudes, but evidence.

Sceptics may ask whether one page can truly matter. Yet constraint is the method's strength. The brevity forces distillation. It leaves no room for rambling narrative or defensive justification. What you choose to write becomes, by necessity, the signal rather than the noise. The one-page debrief cuts to the essence of a cycle's learning: one victory, one wound, one decision worth remembering. That clarity is what sharpens judgment over time.

The practice also changes posture. To write to your future self is to assume continuity—to imagine that you will be here, running this business, facing new but related challenges. That imaginative act plants a subtle seed of resilience. It affirms that today's effort belongs to a longer arc, that your struggles are not isolated moments but chapters in an unfolding enterprise.

Yet there is an unresolved question. How many owners will commit to such a ritual, when the lure of the urgent always outshouts the quiet discipline of reflection? To pause and write feels optional, unbillable, even frivolous. And yet the archive of these letters, once built, reveals itself as the most valuable asset a business can hold—not cash, not tools, but wisdom made visible.

So the deeper challenge is not whether one can write a page, but whether one can believe in its future worth. Will you leave your future self to stumble blind into the same patterns? Or will you send forward a map, written in your own hand, marking the terrain already travelled? The answer lies in whether you will take the time, now, to write that letter—before the lessons of this cycle slip beyond recall.

Chapter 9
Tools, Spreadsheets, and the Minimum Viable Stack

Every generation of business owners has faced the same temptation: to believe that the next tool will finally bring order. In the nineteenth century, factory managers swore by new ledger books with novel columns; in the twentieth, it was the rise of calculators, filing cabinets, and enterprise software. Today, the same promise is whispered from subscription dashboards, AI assistants, and glossy integrations—*just one more tool, and everything will be simple.* Yet the paradox is clear: the more we chase, the less we use. Tools, like diets, only work if we stay with them long enough for results to compound.

The allure of choice is powerful but corrosive. A new app launches, promising a "smarter" way to manage expenses, invoices, or calendars. Forums buzz with reviews. Colleagues enthuse about features you don't have. You sign up, migrate data, fiddle with settings—and then a rival tool emerges, shinier still. This cycle is more than inefficient; it erodes trust in your own systems. Stability never arrives, because you are always building foundations on fresh soil. The overlooked truth is that most businesses could thrive on a short stack of well-used basics, supplemented by spreadsheets that refuse to die because they remain unmatched in flexibility.

The history of business practice suggests a recurring lesson: longevity belongs not to the most feature-rich but to the most graspable. The spreadsheet, first released in 1979 as VisiCalc, revolutionised financial thinking not because it was complex, but because it let managers *see* the numbers, manipulate them, and test scenarios. Forty years on, it remains the quiet backbone of commerce. Against a backdrop of apps promising automation nirvana, the spreadsheet endures because it grants sovereignty: your rules, your format, your exports. To treat it as primitive is to miss its power.

But this chapter is not a hymn to austerity. Tools matter. They accelerate, safeguard, and enable scale. The point is to choose *less but better*—to commit with deliberation and then redirect energy away from endless comparison toward actual execution. A credible invoicing system, a trustworthy bank feed, a shared drive with version control: these are enough to anchor operations. Add to that a set of spreadsheets designed not for beauty but for speed—a profit-and-loss template, a cash calendar, a pricing calculator—and you already possess a functional cockpit. From day one, such a minimal yet coherent stack produces confidence: you can measure, forecast, and decide without drowning in noise.

The deeper question is not technical but philosophical: when is automation an ally, and when does it become a tyrant? Too often, businesses overreach—stringing together fragile webs of integrations that break at midnight, creating more maintenance than they save. The wiser path is proportionate automation: rules that are simple enough to explain on paper, zaps that can be tested in minutes, guardrails that preserve uptime rather than compromise it. Reliability, not novelty, is the metric that matters. The lesson is ancient—engineers have always known that elegance lies not in complexity, but in resilience.

And then there is sovereignty. Vendor risk is no abstraction: a platform can fold, a subscription can spike in cost, a login can be revoked. Without control over your own data, you are a tenant in someone else's house. Monthly exports, clean foldering, and archived spreadsheets are not administrative chores but acts of independence. They guarantee that you can leave one tool for another without crippling downtime. This mindset—of owning, not renting your records—guards against fragility. It means agility is preserved, and panic is replaced with calm.

The scope of this chapter is therefore practical and strategic at once. We will explore how to pick a minimum viable stack without paralysis, how to use starter spreadsheets to win confidence immediately, how to layer automation without crossing into brittleness, and how to safeguard your data with disciplined exits. Each theme returns to a single principle: the measure of a system is not how impressive it looks on launch day, but how faithfully it serves you under pressure.

Yet the tension remains unresolved. If simplicity is the goal, why do so many of us complicate? If sovereignty is possible, why do we surrender control so readily? Perhaps it is because the harder work is not choosing tools, but trusting ourselves to stay with them. That is the invitation ahead: to resist the restless churn of the marketplace and instead build a stack—lean, resilient, and yours—that will endure.

Choose Less, Use More

The modern business owner is drowning in abundance. At any moment, hundreds of apps clamour for attention—each claiming to be the missing piece in the financial puzzle. There is a subscription for invoicing, another for expenses, three more for dashboards, all packaged with glossy interfaces and promises of productivity nirvana. Yet beneath the sheen lies a paradox: the more tools we adopt, the less we use them. Switching, testing, and comparing drains time, erodes focus, and produces instability. Systems are rebuilt again and again, but never trusted long enough for confidence to take root.

Consider a freelancer who spends three evenings researching project management software instead of finalising invoices. She signs up for trials, watches tutorials, exports her old data—only to abandon the new system when the learning curve proves steep. Weeks later, she repeats the cycle with another "better" tool. Revenue is delayed, not because her work lacks quality, but because her attention is misallocated. The real issue is not a shortage of tools but a shortage of commitment. Simplicity, in this context, is not a luxury but a discipline.

The discipline begins with a single decision: choose fewer tools, but use them fully. Imagine narrowing the stack to one accounting system, one drive, and one or two spreadsheets tailored to the essentials. Once chosen, the goal is not to keep shopping but to stop. That act of closure—the refusal to chase novelty—frees attention for the harder, more valuable work: serving clients, improving offers, and steering the business. Using what you already have produces more progress than acquiring what you do not.

The criteria for such choices are not mysterious. They can be boiled down to three: speed, exportability, and rules. Speed matters because financial tools that lag, freeze, or demand endless clicks will be abandoned. Exportability matters because your data is your sovereignty—without clean exports, you are hostage to the platform. Rules matter because tools must fit your workflows rather than dictate them; a system that resists your way of working will eventually be discarded. These three benchmarks—quick to use, easy to leave, respectful of your rules—are the quiet foundation of durability.

Against this framework, spreadsheets reveal their enduring power. A simple cash calendar in Excel or Google Sheets can outstrip a dozen cash flow apps, not because it dazzles with features, but because it bends to your logic, exports cleanly, and never locks you in. A P&L template built once can be reused indefinitely, evolving with your needs instead of being replaced wholesale. The spreadsheet, for all its plainness, satisfies the three criteria more consistently than most specialist software. It is not an accident that even billion-pound firms continue to rely on it in the background: it is a universal language of numbers.

Yet the temptation to abandon the plain for the shiny is persistent. App developers thrive on promising efficiency gains that rarely materialise. The cost is not merely subscription fees but cognitive drag. Every new tool imposes migration overhead, resets habits, and creates fragility when integrations break. In contrast, a restrained approach compounds value. Familiarity deepens. Processes stabilise. What once felt clumsy becomes second nature, and fluency replaces friction.

There is also a psychological dimension. When a business owner repeatedly switches systems, they internalise a sense of instability—*my tools are not right, therefore I am not ready*. By contrast, choosing once and committing reinforces confidence. It is a subtle but powerful shift: instead of seeing systems as a permanent experiment, they are trusted as infrastructure. Just as a craftsman grows into their tools, so too does a business grow into its chosen stack.

Still, restraint is not rigidity. Committing to a core system does not mean ignoring innovation forever. It means setting a high bar for change: only switching when the benefit is undeniable, the export path is smooth, and the rules of use are preserved. This guardrail ensures that evolution is deliberate, not reactive. The paradox resolves: progress comes not from maximising choice, but from minimising churn.

What emerges is a philosophy of enough. A few credible tools and a spreadsheet path—chosen for speed, exportability, and rules—are sufficient to run a resilient business. From that base, stability appears, not because the tools are perfect, but because they are used. The friction of endless comparison fades. The work of building a company regains its centrality.

Yet a lingering tension remains. If choosing less and using more is so clearly effective, why do so many persist in the chase? Perhaps because commitment feels riskier than exploration. To choose once is to give up the fantasy that perfection lies just around the corner. But in that surrender lies freedom—the freedom to work, to trust, and to let stability compound. The question is whether we can resist the lure of novelty long enough to find it.

Starter Spreadsheet Pack

Every revolution begins not with a grand system but with a simple tool in the right hands. For business owners, that tool is often a spreadsheet. Humble in appearance, it carries a paradoxical power: from the most basic grid of rows and columns, entire companies are steered. Yet, in an age of specialised software, many overlook the spreadsheet's quiet strength. It does not dazzle, but it endures. It does not lock you in, but it gives you clarity. For a company of one, it may be the most effective financial stack available.

Picture the contrast. One entrepreneur spends weeks evaluating accounting apps, toggling between features, debating subscriptions. Another downloads three pre-prepared spreadsheets: a profit-and-loss tracker, a cash calendar, and a pricing calculator. Within an afternoon, she has recorded her income, mapped her outflows, and tested a service package's profitability. She is not paralysed by choice. She is already operational. By day one, she is building confidence rather than chasing tools.

At its heart, the starter spreadsheet pack is not about technology—it is about rhythm. Numbers are not useful when buried in complexity, but when integrated into the cycle of decision-making. The P&L sheet captures the heartbeat: income earned, expenses spent, the net result in black or red. The cash calendar turns that static figure into motion: when money is expected in, when bills are due out, how peaks and troughs align. The pricing calculator closes the loop: every decision about what to sell is grounded not in guesswork but in evidence of time costs, contribution margins, and breakeven points.

Each of these tools addresses a universal friction point. The P&L tackles the common blindness of "busy but broke"—when sales feel high yet net earnings vanish. By recording income and outflows consistently, the sheet reveals whether growth is real or illusory. The cash calendar answers the entrepreneur's most sleepless question: *will I have enough to cover what's due?* Instead of vague worry, there is a dated map. The pricing calculator prevents undercharging by exposing the true cost of delivery, forcing a confrontation between ambition and arithmetic.

Simplicity here does not mean weakness. A well-designed P&L sheet can rival the insight of a full accounting platform if used with discipline. A cash calendar in a spreadsheet can highlight risks before they metastasise into crises, because it is tuned to the owner's lived reality rather than hidden in software menus. And a pricing calculator, modest though it looks, may be the single most transformative tool—because it not only protects margins but reshapes how an owner values their own time.

Examples bring this alive. A consultant realises, through her P&L sheet, that while revenue from workshops appears healthy, travel and preparation costs erode almost half the margin. She chooses to retire that service and focus on retainer clients. A designer, running his cash calendar, notices that invoices sent at month's end always cause a mid-month crunch. He shifts his rhythm: invoices go out mid-month, receipts stabilise, and the crunch vanishes. A coach, armed with her pricing calculator, recognises that her entry-level package consumes double the hours she assumed. She raises the fee. Clients stay. For the first time, she pays herself predictably.

The psychological impact of such small wins is profound. Once an owner sees results within hours—not months—the inertia of "someday I'll get my finances organised" breaks. Momentum replaces hesitation. Confidence is not abstract; it is grounded in tangible numbers visible on a single sheet. By making the invisible visible, the starter pack lowers anxiety and raises agency.

Critics may argue that spreadsheets are fragile, that errors creep in, that automation is limited. And they are right, if the sheet is poorly designed or misused. But the answer is not to abandon spreadsheets entirely. It is to begin with tested templates, aligned with the core loops of P&L, cash flow, and pricing. For a business of one, sophistication is not complexity but fit. The spreadsheet's beauty is that it grows with you: formulas can be added, tabs expanded, dashboards layered in—but only when you are ready.

There is also a deeper philosophical thread. A spreadsheet forces a kind of intimacy with your numbers that software can obscure. You see the cells, the calculations, the links. There is no magic behind the curtain. This transparency cultivates not only understanding but ownership. It is one thing to be told your margin is 30 per cent. It is another to see the subtraction row that proves it. That visibility transforms numbers from abstractions into decisions.

The starter pack also offers resilience. In a world where SaaS tools rise and fall, where platforms change pricing tiers or collapse entirely, a spreadsheet remains yours. Data is portable, exports are trivial, and no vendor holds you hostage. In this way, the spreadsheet embodies sovereignty: your financial record is not rented but owned. For a small business, that sovereignty is not academic—it is survival.

Day-one wins are not trivial. They create a pattern of early trust. The first time you see a P&L that reconciles, the first time your cash calendar predicts a pinch and you avert it, the first time a calculator justifies a higher fee—you cross from reaction to direction. From that point, the system reinforces itself. Confidence compounds cycle by cycle.

And yet, the paradox remains. If a spreadsheet can be so powerful, why do so many skip it for tools that promise more? Perhaps because complexity is seductive; it feels more professional to use a platform with a dashboard than a grid of cells. But what appears sophisticated often conceals fragility. The truth is starker: stability is built not on features but on use. And few tools are used as fully, as flexibly, and as enduringly as a spreadsheet.

The question, then, is not whether the starter spreadsheet pack is enough—it almost always is. The real question is whether we can trust simplicity long enough for its compounding benefits to show. To choose it is to commit to clarity over novelty, evidence over promises, and practice over procrastination. Perhaps the spreadsheet, dismissed as ordinary, is precisely the foundation extraordinary businesses require.

Automation Without Overreach

The seduction of automation is easy to understand. With a few clicks, the promise is clear: hours of drudgery erased, flows of data dancing between tools, and a business that hums on autopilot. Yet behind that promise lies a paradox. For every entrepreneur whose carefully built automations quietly amplify their output, another has a system collapse spectacularly—an invoice mis-sent, a client email vanishing into a misfired zap, or a payment feed duplicated until accounts no longer reconcile. Automation offers leverage, but without restraint, it breeds fragility.

One striking example is the small consultancy that, flush with enthusiasm for efficiency, built a chain of 27 automated rules: invoices triggered by time logs, reminders firing into Slack, receipts fed directly into folders. For a month, it worked beautifully. Then one broken link—an expired API token—brought the entire system down. Hours were spent untangling the mess, correcting errors, explaining to clients. What was designed to free time ended up consuming more of it. The lesson was not that automation is dangerous, but that automation without boundaries creates hidden liabilities.

The principle is simple: automation should scale with complexity, not outrun it. A solo business or small team thrives when each rule or integration earns its place, tested not only for speed but also for reliability and resilience. A zap that sends receipts to cloud storage is almost unbreakable. A rule that triggers payments across multiple platforms is brittle by design. The first adds confidence. The second adds hidden risk. Automation is not about how much can be automated but how much should.

The first guardrail is thresholding. Only automate what you already understand manually. If you cannot describe a process in three steps on paper, it is not ready to be automated. Too many owners skip this stage, automating chaos instead of order. The result is amplified confusion. Better to start with one simple feed—say, auto-forwarding bank notifications into a tracking folder—than to leap into chaining multiple apps. Mastery builds from the ground up.

Another guardrail is exportability. Every automated system should have an exit route: the ability to pause, to download, to revert to manual if required. Without this, you are hostage to vendors and integrations. A fragile system often shows itself when the owner admits, "If this breaks, I wouldn't know where to start." Robust automation, by contrast, always comes with a fallback. It works for you, but you remain in control.

Consider the psychological impact of automation, too. Used wisely, it reduces cognitive load. A business owner no longer worries about filing receipts or updating cash forecasts because those tasks flow automatically. Anxiety falls. But when overreach sets in, the opposite occurs: the owner is now responsible not only for their business but also for maintaining a complex, invisible system. Every email becomes a test—did the automation fire? Every delay breeds suspicion—did the zap fail? Stress shifts but does not disappear.

The broader question automation raises is philosophical. Efficiency is often mistaken for progress, but the two are not synonymous. An entrepreneur who saves an hour with brittle automations may still lose the strategic clarity that comes from handling key data manually. A weekly reconciliation done by hand, for instance, is not wasted time; it is an exercise in awareness. Automating it prematurely might remove the learning that comes from seeing how cash moves in real time. The aim is not to remove yourself from the system entirely, but to remove only the noise that distracts from decisions.

Examples of balance illuminate the point. A designer uses automation to categorise and file invoices automatically—no risk, pure gain. But he resists automating client communication beyond templated drafts; trust, he knows, is too precious to hand over to an algorithm. A coach creates a simple zap to archive Zoom recordings into labelled folders—hours saved across the year. Yet she avoids automating her pricing calculator, preferring to revisit it manually, precisely because each calculation forces her to reconsider value and cost. In both cases, restraint proves as valuable as ingenuity.

The temptation, of course, is always to push further. Once one workflow is humming, another cries out to be automated. But each step requires a test: will this make the system more reliable or more brittle? Will uptime rise or risk accumulate? The answers demand not technical expertise but managerial wisdom—the ability to resist overreach. In this sense, automation becomes not a technical project but a discipline of judgment.

The motif that runs through all of this is proportion. Just as a bridge must be engineered to carry expected loads without overbuilding into waste or underbuilding into collapse, so must a business's automations be sized to its stage and needs. Proportion is not static; it evolves. What begins as a single zap may, in a year, grow into a small network. But growth must be earned. Complexity must stay tethered to reliability.

The question for every owner is therefore not "what else can I automate?" but "what should stay human?" Which processes benefit from rules and feeds, and which are richer when touched directly? The spreadsheet that updates itself may be helpful, but the end-of-month debrief letter must be written by hand. Efficiency here would strip away meaning. The tension remains unresolved: how far can we lean on automation without hollowing out the very awareness that keeps us in control?

Perhaps the truest discipline lies in restraint. To use automation not as an escape from work but as a reinforcement of stability. To let systems run, but never so far that we forget how to run them ourselves. The promise of automation is not freedom from responsibility—it is freedom to focus on the decisions that only humans can make. The real challenge is knowing when enough is enough.

Backups and Exits

The end of the nineteenth century saw entire companies collapse not because their products failed, but because their records burned. In an age before digital redundancy, one warehouse fire could erase invoices, payroll logs, and customer histories in an afternoon. The business ceased not for lack of demand but for lack of memory. A century later, the threat looks different but the essence is the same: reliance on a single fragile repository—whether a cloud tool, a vendor's server, or an unbacked laptop—leaves the owner's sovereignty at risk.

Modern entrepreneurs assume the cloud is permanent. Dropbox, Google Drive, QuickBooks, Xero—these services appear monolithic, eternal. Yet companies disappear, policies shift, logins are locked, and integrations break. One consultant tells of waking to find their accounting platform shut down overnight after a buyout; years of invoices and reconciliations sat in limbo, accessible only through a tedious extraction process. Another recalls a subscription tool doubling its fees, leaving the choice between paying far more than planned or abandoning workflows overnight. In each case, the owner had mistaken convenience for permanence. The cost of that illusion was dependence.

Data sovereignty is not an abstract legal principle; it is the lived ability to pick up your history and walk away. Exporting your records—monthly, without fail—transforms dependence into resilience. A CSV of your client list, a PDF archive of invoices, a simple copy of bank feeds: these are not glamorous artefacts, but they are lifeboats. They ensure that your business remains yours, even if a vendor ceases to exist or simply ceases to serve you well.

The discipline of backups is deceptively modest. A monthly export feels unnecessary when everything is working, much like insurance feels unnecessary until the accident. Yet the value compounds invisibly. A library of exports across twelve months is more than a failsafe; it is a rolling archive that grants perspective. The business owner can look back at decisions, track subtle shifts, and rebuild narratives that memory alone would distort. What looks like overhead becomes the foundation of clarity.

There is also a philosophical dimension here: agility is not the absence of tools but the ability to leave them. A business trapped in a single platform is not agile; it is captive. The most resilient owners cultivate optionality, knowing that choice itself is power. They do not chase novelty endlessly, but neither do they mistake stability for permanence. By exporting, archiving, and maintaining clean exits, they preserve the one advantage every small business has over larger institutions: the freedom to change course quickly.

Consider two contrasting stories. A coach running her practice on a cloud CRM spends thirty minutes each month exporting her client notes and payment history. When the service changes its terms, she switches to a rival within a week, clients unaffected, continuity preserved. A designer, by contrast, builds his pricing models, contracts, and accounts inside a bespoke app that offers no export. When it shutters, he loses years of data overnight and scrambles to reconstruct the essentials. Both had the same tools. Only one treated them as temporary scaffolding rather than permanent shelter.

The temptation, especially in the early years, is to defer this discipline. "I'll export later." "This vendor is stable." "Switching is unthinkable." These are comforting fictions. No vendor, however credible, is immune to disruption. Nor is any system immune to your own future needs evolving beyond it. The exit you ignore today is the lock-in you regret tomorrow.

What is striking is how little effort sovereignty requires. A calendar reminder, a single export button, a folder labelled "Archive YYYY-MM." The friction is measured in minutes. The payoff is measured in freedom. The business that owns its data outright can switch accountants, upgrade tools, or pause operations without panic. The one that does not finds itself negotiating from weakness, its own history hostage to another's system.

At heart, backups and exits are less about technology than about mindset. They are a posture of humility in the face of change: a recognition that no system lasts forever, that certainty is temporary, and that stewardship demands foresight. For the solo founder or small team, this posture translates into stability. For the careless, its absence translates into fragility.

The lingering question, then, is not whether you can trust your tools, but whether you can trust yourself to leave them. Have you built a business that can migrate at will, carrying its records like a passport, or have you unknowingly tied your fortunes to a vendor's uptime and goodwill? Freedom in business is not won by automation or growth alone. It is won by the quiet, deliberate act of keeping your exit open.

Chapter 10
From Numbers to Narrative: Running the Business You Want

There is a subtle but profound difference between knowing where your business stands and knowing where you want it to take you. The first is a matter of arithmetic; the second, of authorship. The ledger can tell you what happened—revenues earned, expenses spent, hours billed, cash banked. But left unexamined, those numbers are inert: a snapshot of the past rather than a compass for the future. The moment they are woven into a story—about capacity, fit, energy, sustainability—they stop being sterile figures and become evidence, a narrative thread pointing toward the business you actually want to run.

Consider the paradox that animates so many independent careers: ambition runs hot, but capacity runs cool. A freelancer resolves to double revenue within a year, yet their rolling twelve months of data suggest a growth trajectory closer to twenty per cent. Which is more valuable—the dream or the discipline? The answer is not either-or. Anchoring goals in evidence does not extinguish ambition; it hardens it into something sturdier. The motivation of chasing a credible target, set in light of actual base rates, outlasts the sugar rush of fantasy. In this sense, financial data is not the enemy of vision but its ballast.

Numbers alone, however, do not dictate a life worth living. A business is not only a machine for producing cash but a portfolio of work that shapes its owner's days. Some projects fatten margins but drain spirit; others pay modestly yet ignite joy. Without a system for weighing both dimensions, the business slips into ad-hoc acceptance—whatever comes, comes. The discipline of curating work with both profit and energy in view transforms that drift into direction. A client roster becomes not just a set of contracts but a designed mix, aligned with values as well as economics. This is where margin and meaning intersect.

Tied to this is a perennial dilemma: when to say no, and when to seek help. Many small businesses run on heroics until exhaustion makes the decision for them. Burnout, however, is not proof of strength but of failed capacity management. By treating thresholds—hours, margins, workload—as quantifiable signals, decisions gain clarity. Should you subcontract? Raise prices? Turn work away? These questions shift from agonising improvisations to guided choices. Sustainability, in this light, is not a matter of personality but of policy, a discipline in which health and profit are no longer adversaries but allies.

Threaded through all of this is the possibility of something rare: a calm operating system. Not a grand framework imposed from outside, but a living rhythm built from weekly, monthly, and quarterly cycles. The numbers feed the story, the story guides the choices, and the choices reinforce the cycles. Confidence, then, is not conjured; it is earned. The business begins to feel less like a series of emergencies and more like a coherent organism—stable, light, and free.

The stakes of this chapter are not technical but existential. It asks: what does it mean to run the business you *want*, rather than the business that happens to you? It offers no grandiose promise of control, but something subtler: the ability to steer with evidence, to design with intent, to exit the loop of constant reaction. What follows is not a script but a set of tools and lenses through which the numbers of your business can be read as the narrative of your life. The reader who embraces this shift may find that the data they once feared becomes the most humanising force of all.

And yet, a tension lingers. Evidence disciplines ambition, but can it also dampen it? Systems foster calm, but can they inadvertently reduce spontaneity? What is the balance between steering by numbers and leaving room for surprise? Those questions remain open. The pages ahead will not settle them finally, but they will arm you with the clarity to face them directly. For it is only by mastering the story our numbers tell that we gain the chance to write one of our own choosing.

Goal Setting That Respects Reality

Every January, business owners write down goals with the kind of optimism usually reserved for marathon runners at the starting line. "Double revenue. Triple output. Launch three new products." The air hums with ambition. Yet by March, the same entrepreneurs find themselves falling behind, wondering where the gap lies between what they hoped and what they could actually deliver. The paradox is stark: goals are supposed to inspire, yet unrealistic ones often corrode morale. What begins as a promise of growth can end as a weight of failure.

The great error lies not in having ambition but in mistaking it for capacity. Ambition sets direction, but capacity sets pace. When the two are misaligned, plans unravel. The discipline of anchoring goals to reality is less about trimming dreams and more about ensuring they can survive contact with the calendar. Evidence—base rates from one's sector, rolling-twelve data from one's own books—provides that anchor. It transforms targets from slogans into commitments that can be executed and sustained.

Consider the small design studio that projected 100 per cent growth after its first successful year. The partners worked twelve-hour days, weekends included, chasing the ambitious figure. But when they reviewed their rolling twelve months of billings, the truth was obvious: their growth rate was closer to twenty per cent, and even that had required overextension. They were not underperforming; they had simply chosen a fantasy as a benchmark. Resetting their goals to align with base rates in their industry—and with their own operational rhythm—did not dampen their motivation. On the contrary, it replaced fatigue with momentum. The aim shifted from chasing an illusion to building steadily, compounding reliably.

Rolling-twelve data deserves particular attention. Annual targets often conceal seasonality, one-off anomalies, or end-of-year surges. A rolling-twelve view neutralises these distortions, capturing a living average that reflects ongoing reality. If, for example, your consultancy earned £240,000 in the twelve months ending in June, that is a sturdier foundation for projecting the next twelve months than simply doubling the £40,000 you happened to make in December. Evidence replaces hope as the unit of planning.

There is also a psychological dividend. Goals grounded in reality are not only more credible—they are more motivating. Few things drain energy faster than chasing an outcome you quietly suspect is impossible. By contrast, a credible stretch target—slightly above your historical trajectory, but achievable with disciplined effort—creates a virtuous cycle of effort and reward. The human mind thrives on progress that feels both challenging and within reach.

Yet here lies the tension: ambition has its place. Without it, businesses stagnate. The challenge is not to choose between ambition and realism, but to let evidence mediate between them. This mediation produces sturdier motivation, the kind that can withstand setbacks. To return to our marathon metaphor: the runner who paces themselves according to their training data is more likely to finish strongly than the one who sprints the first ten miles on adrenaline.

Modern tools make this discipline easier. Cloud-based accounting systems can generate rolling-twelve profit and loss statements in seconds. Industry benchmarks are published by trade associations, consultancy firms, and even government statistics agencies. The data is out there. The obstacle is often not access but willingness—the humility to accept what the evidence says, even when it clashes with our desire for rapid breakthroughs.

This humility has philosophical weight. To respect reality is to respect time, limits, and the cost of human effort. It acknowledges that motivation is not strengthened by fantasy but by credibility. A target that reflects capacity is a kind of contract with the future self: "I will not set you up for burnout; I will set you up for progress." In this sense, evidence-based goals are acts of care, not constraint.

And yet, a question lingers. If we allow evidence to dictate every target, do we risk dulling our capacity for boldness? Might we trade possibility for predictability? Perhaps. But the more pressing danger for most small businesses is the opposite: ignoring evidence until reality imposes itself in harsher form—missed payrolls, broken commitments, exhaustion. The art, then, is not to abandon ambition, but to frame it within the bounds of reality so it can endure.

Numbers are not enemies of vision. They are its allies—its guardrails, its stabilisers, its silent truth-tellers. Anchoring goals to rolling-twelve data and base rates does not shrink ambition; it matures it. And perhaps the more provocative question is this: once your goals are credible, how much more daring could your actions become—because you finally believe they can hold?

Designing an Intentional Work Mix

Every business owner can recall a project that looked harmless when it arrived but turned corrosive over time. The margins were slim, the client was demanding, and the work consumed far more energy than it returned. On paper, the numbers might have been tolerable. In practice, the project drained both profit and spirit. At the other end of the spectrum are assignments that feel almost effortless: they pay fairly, align with personal values, and leave the practitioner energised rather than depleted. The paradox is plain: two projects of identical financial value can have radically different impacts on the health of a business.

The temptation is to treat all revenue as equally good, as though money has no texture. But this mindset locks many sole proprietors into cycles of exhaustion and resentment. The antidote is a more nuanced measure: margin and joy, side by side. Margin reveals the financial yield; joy measures the emotional return. Together, they provide a map for designing a portfolio of work that is not only profitable but sustainable. In an era where burnout stalks even the most talented professionals, this dual lens offers not luxury but necessity.

Consider the case of a freelance copywriter who divided her projects into four quadrants: high margin/high joy, high margin/low joy, low margin/high joy, and low margin/low joy. The first quadrant—profitable and enjoyable—became her anchor. The second—profitable but draining—was tolerated only in small doses. The third—fun but underpaid—was reclassified as pro bono or hobby.

And the fourth, predictably, was eliminated. Over a year, this matrix reshaped her practice. The effect was profound: not only did her income rise, but her days felt lighter, her creativity sharper. The mere act of classifying work had surfaced hidden truths about her choices.

This approach draws from portfolio theory in finance, where investors diversify not just by return but by risk. Here, the investor is the business owner, and the assets are projects. Each client or assignment carries its own blend of profit and emotional cost. Viewed individually, the trade-offs may seem minor. Viewed collectively, patterns emerge—some projects subsidise others, some erode overall performance. The shift from ad-hoc acceptance to portfolio view transforms reactive survival into deliberate strategy.

Exiting low-fit work smoothly is as important as selecting the right mix. Many hesitate to disengage from clients who are unprofitable or joyless, fearing conflict or income loss. Yet the act of letting go is often liberating. A designer who consistently underpriced services for a legacy client finally raised rates to market standard. The client declined, and the contract ended. Within weeks, the designer filled the slot with a higher-paying, more aligned client. What felt like risk proved to be an upgrade disguised as loss. The principle is stark: capacity spent on misfit work blocks capacity for fit.

The deeper philosophical insight is this: work is not neutral. It shapes the worker as much as the balance sheet. To curate work intentionally is to assert that profit and energy should rise together. One without the other is unsustainable. Chasing only margin leads to hollow victories—wealth without vitality. Chasing only joy risks financial fragility. The intersection is where enduring businesses are built.

Practical tools can support this intentionality. A simple spreadsheet can track projects against both margin and joy scores. Over time, averages reveal trends: perhaps creative agency work consistently scores high on joy but low on margin; perhaps corporate contracts deliver margin but little joy. With data in hand, decisions acquire clarity. This clarity, in turn, tempers the volatility of mood. One bad week no longer defines the business; the portfolio speaks louder than any single project.

Still, tension persists. Should one always optimise for both joy and margin? Or are there seasons where one must dominate—taking on less joyful work to stabilise finances, or accepting slimmer margins to pursue deeply meaningful projects? These questions have no formulaic answer. They demand judgment, context, and a willingness to trade short-term imbalance for long-term design. The key is not to eliminate trade-offs but to choose them consciously.

Ultimately, designing an intentional work mix is less about spreadsheets than about sovereignty. It is the refusal to let accident dictate livelihood. It is a stance: that work should nourish as well as reward, align with values as well as bank accounts. Yet a provocative question remains. If margin and joy are the twin guides, what happens when they point in opposite directions—when the most lucrative work threatens to corrode the very energy that sustains it? To live by the numbers alone would be folly, but to live by joy alone is equally fragile. The enduring challenge—and perhaps the mark of mastery—is learning how to balance these two measures, not once, but again and again, as the seasons of business unfold.

When to Say No, When to Hire Help

There is a moment in almost every small business where success begins to look suspiciously like failure. The phone keeps ringing, invoices multiply, and yet exhaustion seeps in at the edges. The paradox is cruel: what you once longed for—more work, more clients, more recognition—now threatens to undo you. The unspoken truth is that growth carries hidden costs, and unless they are recognised and managed, they can hollow out both profit and health.

One consultant described the turning point vividly: "I realised I had become my own worst boss—demanding, relentless, and impossible to please. I was earning more than before, but I was constantly behind, constantly tired." What she lacked was not discipline but a framework for choice. The real question was not whether to work harder but whether to draw a line: either decline certain opportunities or expand capacity by bringing in others. The art lies in knowing when to say no and when to hire help.

The first step in this art is quantification. Vague impressions of being "too busy" or "overwhelmed" are easy to dismiss. Numbers, however, refuse to be ignored. For example, if a project will take forty hours, and your available weekly hours are thirty, the shortfall is clear. You can either refuse the work, renegotiate scope, raise prices, or subcontract. The decision becomes less about guilt or emotion and more about arithmetic. In this way, saying no is not an act of weakness but of clarity.

Yet numbers alone do not solve the dilemma. There is a deeper tension: reputation versus sustainability. Saying yes to everything may protect short-term reputation—appearing accommodating, always available—but corrodes long-term sustainability. Saying no may feel risky, but it preserves energy for higher-fit opportunities. A photographer, for instance, who declined constant low-paying event work freed capacity to pursue corporate contracts that paid triple. The no, in retrospect, was not loss but strategy.

Hiring help introduces another layer of complexity. Many resist subcontracting, fearing quality control issues or the discomfort of handing over client-facing work. Yet there is a threshold where refusal to delegate becomes self-sabotage. A web developer who insists on coding every line personally will eventually face diminishing returns: too many projects, not enough hours. By bringing in a trusted subcontractor for the repeatable tasks, the developer preserves capacity for higher-value design and client strategy. The profit margin on subcontracted work may be smaller, but the overall revenue and sustainability of the practice expand.

The decision tree, then, is deceptively simple: if work exceeds capacity and cannot be made profitable at current pricing, you either raise prices, subcontract, or decline. Each option carries consequences, but indecision is the most costly of all. What begins as manageable overwork can evolve into burnout, and burnout is not just an emotional state—it is a capacity problem. No business, however profitable on paper, can outlast a consistently exhausted operator.

This recognition reframes sustainability from a personal indulgence to a policy. Sustainability is not the opposite of ambition; it is ambition's ally. By embedding thresholds—hours per week, margin per project, energy scores—you build a system that protects both profit and health. The business becomes less reactive and more intentional. A "yes" is no longer automatic but earned; a "no" no longer feels like failure but like stewardship of finite resources.

There is also a cultural dimension here. Many solo operators carry inherited scripts: that saying no is rude, that delegation signals incompetence, that real professionals never turn work away. These scripts need dismantling. In practice, the strongest businesses are those that prune as much as they grow, that curate as much as they chase. Saying no is not a sign of weakness but of discernment. Hiring help is not dilution but amplification. Both are forms of control, reclaimed from the chaos of unexamined growth.

Philosophically, the choice comes down to coherence. Do your decisions align with the kind of business—and life—you claim to want? If the goal is stability, then chronic overextension is incoherent. If the goal is impact, then drowning in low-fit work is incoherent. The coherence test is simple yet demanding: each yes and each hire should move you closer to a business that nourishes rather than drains.

And yet the question persists, unresolved and perhaps unresolvable: how do you know in advance which no will open space for something better, and which hire will truly expand rather than entangle? The decision tree provides logic, but logic cannot remove uncertainty. Every "no" carries opportunity cost; every subcontract carries risk. The only certainty is that avoiding the choice—hoping to manage everything alone—extracts the highest price of all. To build a business that endures, one must embrace the discomfort of these choices, again and again, as the seasons shift and capacity is tested anew.

The Calm Operating System

There is a peculiar irony in entrepreneurship: the very freedom that draws people in often collapses into chaos once the business begins to breathe on its own. A single missed invoice, a half-forgotten receipt, or a hurried decision snowballs into a week spent firefighting rather than creating. What starts as a vision of independence becomes a pattern of constant reaction. Yet the businesses that last are rarely the ones fuelled by adrenaline; they are those that learn to run on calm.

Calm does not mean idle, nor does it imply the absence of ambition. Rather, it signals a deliberate architecture—an operating system—that replaces improvisation with rhythm. Consider the analogy of a jazz quartet: the freedom to improvise exists only because of the underlying structure, the agreed key, the steady time. Without that, noise replaces music. In the same way, a business without cycles and rituals feels frantic; with them, it can feel light, even playful, precisely because the essentials are already held by the system.

The core of such a system is the loop: the repeating weekly, monthly, and quarterly cycles that anchor decision-making. Weekly reviews provide granularity—the texture of cash inflows, outflows, pipeline shifts, and commitments. Monthly closes zoom out to reveal patterns invisible in the day-to-day turbulence. Quarterly themes offer an even broader lens, distilling lessons into direction. Each level of the loop reinforces the others, so that no single period holds the entire burden of clarity. Instead, clarity accumulates.

What makes this operating system *calm* is not the absence of effort but the removal of unnecessary friction. A ledger reviewed weekly prevents the surprise of unpaid invoices. A cash calendar inspected monthly prevents panic before tax deadlines. A quarterly debrief, written like a letter to one's future self, prevents drift and repetition of past mistakes. Each ritual is small, but together they create a sense of stability that is greater than the sum of its parts. The mind relaxes because the system remembers.

Of course, some resist systematisation, fearing it will strangle creativity or weigh down agility. The opposite is true. The calm operating system does not dictate what you must do; it ensures that what you have already chosen is visible and honest. It acts as a mirror more than a leash. A designer might discover, through a three-month review, that the most draining client delivers the thinnest margin. A coach may see that referrals spike after publishing content, not after chasing leads. These insights do not lock you in—they free you from illusion.

Consider the effect on confidence. Without structure, confidence is fragile, dependent on mood or luck. With structure, confidence roots itself in proof. It is one thing to hope you can afford a new hire; it is another to see, in the rolling twelve-month data, that cash flows and margins can support it. It is one thing to believe you are improving; it is another to see trends in revenue per client rising quarter over quarter. Confidence born of evidence is quieter, less boastful, but far harder to shake.

There is also a moral dimension. The ledger, when engaged with consistently, keeps you honest. It strips away the self-deception of being "busy but broke." It prevents the comforting delusion that volume equals viability. And paradoxically, it grants freedom—because freedom without honesty is unsustainable. By confronting the numbers regularly, you avoid the slow erosion of trust in yourself and in your business.

The calm operating system is therefore less about software than about philosophy. Tools matter, but their purpose is only to support the loop. Rituals matter, but their purpose is only to anchor attention. What ultimately defines calm is alignment: between values and practice, between ambition and capacity, between decision and data. A business that hums in this way feels lighter, not because the work has vanished, but because the weight is distributed across cycles, processes, and habits that carry it reliably.

And yet, a question lingers. If calm is so powerful, why do so many resist it, defaulting instead to cycles of overextension and crisis? Perhaps it is because chaos flatters us—it makes us feel indispensable, heroic even. Calm, by contrast, is humbler. It whispers rather than shouts. To embrace it is to trade the drama of survival for the quieter satisfaction of stewardship. The choice is not obvious, but it is decisive: will your business be sustained by adrenaline, or will it learn to hum on calm?

About the Author

Evelyn Hawthorne writes for the working solitude of small enterprises—the designers, coaches, bakers, and coders who keep their own ledgers and carry their own risk. Her work sits where numbers meet judgement, turning accounts into narratives that help ordinary people make better choices about work, time, and money. A long admirer of Victorian thrift books and early merchant manuals, she believes the smallest books can carry the greatest calm. She splits her weeks between conversations with one-person businesses and the quiet labour of refining simple routines that outlast fashion, offering warm authority: fewer buzzwords, more margins that pay your bills.

www.ingramcontent.com/pod-product-compliance
Lightning Source LLC
Chambersburg PA
CBHW031351230926
51848CB00002B/474
9789374122877